Germany

Everything You Need to Know

Copyright © 2024 by Noah Gil-Smith.

All rights reserved. No part of this book may be reproduced, distributed, or transmitted in any form or by any means, including photocopying, recording, or other electronic or mechanical methods, without the prior written permission of the publisher, except in the case of brief quotations embodied in critical reviews and certain other noncommercial uses permitted by copyright law. This book was created with the assistance of Artificial Intelligence. The content presented in this book is for entertainment purposes only. It should not be considered as a substitute for professional advice or comprehensive research. Readers are encouraged to independently verify any information and consult relevant experts for specific matters. The author and publisher disclaim any liability or responsibility for any loss, injury, or inconvenience caused or alleged to be caused directly or indirectly by the information presented in this book.

Introduction to Germany 6

Germany's Geographical Diversity: From Mountains to Coastlines 8

Early German History: From Ancient Tribes to Holy Roman Empire 10

The Rise and Fall of Prussia: Shaping Modern Germany 12

World Wars and Their Impact on Germany 14

Post-War Germany: Division and Reunification 17

Contemporary German Politics and Government 20

German Economy: Engineering Powerhouse and Global Player 23

German Education System: Excellence and Efficiency 26

German Language: A Key to Understanding Culture and Society 29

Exploring German Wildlife: From the Black Forest to the Baltic Sea 32

Savory Delights: A Culinary Journey Through German Cuisine 34

Berlin: Germany's Vibrant Capital and Historical Center 37

Munich: Bavaria's Heartbeat and Oktoberfest Hub 39

Hamburg: Port City Splendor and Maritime Heritage 42

Frankfurt: Financial Hub and Modern Skyline 44

Cologne: Gothic Splendor and Rhine River Charm 47

Heidelberg: Romanticism and Scholarly Legacy 50

Dresden: Baroque Beauty Rising from the Ashes 53

Leipzig: Music, Literature, and Cultural Crossroads 55

Nuremberg: Medieval Majesty and Modern Resilience 58

Stuttgart: Automotive Innovation and Swabian Hospitality 61

German Art and Architecture: From Romanticism to Bauhaus 63

Music and Literature: German Contributions to World Culture 65

Christmas Markets: Festive Traditions and Holiday Cheer 68

Oktoberfest: Celebrating Bavarian Culture and Beer 71

German Folklore and Fairy Tales: Stories That Transcend Time 73

Castles and Palaces: Fairytale Architecture and Historical Significance 75

Black Forest: Mystical Landscapes and Outdoor Adventures 77

Rhine Valley: Romantic Landscapes and Vineyard Scenery 79

Bavarian Alps: Majestic Peaks and Alpine Wonders 81

German Festivals: From Wine Festivals to Beer Gardens 83

German Fashion and Design: Style with Precision and Elegance 85

German Engineering: Precision and Innovation in Industry 87

German Automotive Industry: A Legacy of Performance and Reliability 90

Beer Culture: Brewing Traditions and Beer Gardens 92

Wine Culture: Vineyard Tours and Riesling Delights 94

German Etiquette and Customs: Navigating Social Norms 96

Efficiency and Punctuality: German Work Ethic in Practice 99

Environmentalism in Germany: Green Policies and Sustainability Efforts 101

Public Transportation: Efficiency and Accessibility Across the Country 103

German Technology: Innovations Shaping the Future 105

German Influence on Global Affairs: Diplomacy and Leadership 108

Epilogue 110

Introduction to Germany

Welcome to the fascinating world of Germany, a country brimming with rich history, vibrant culture, and breathtaking landscapes. Situated in the heart of Europe, Germany has long been a central player in the continent's political, economic, and cultural arenas. From its bustling cities to its picturesque countryside, Germany offers a diverse array of experiences for visitors and residents alike.

With a population of over 80 million people, Germany is the most populous country in the European Union and boasts a highly developed economy that ranks among the largest in the world. Its capital, Berlin, serves as a dynamic hub of creativity, innovation, and historical significance, while cities like Munich, Hamburg, and Frankfurt contribute their own unique flavors to the German tapestry.

Germany's history is as complex as it is fascinating. From ancient tribes and medieval kingdoms to the modern nation-state we know today, the story of Germany is one of triumphs, tragedies, and transformations. Over the centuries, Germany has been home to great thinkers, artists, scientists, and leaders who have left an indelible mark on the world.

The country's landscape is equally diverse, ranging from the towering peaks of the Bavarian Alps to the rolling hills of the Black Forest and the sweeping plains of the North German Plain. Its natural beauty is complemented by a wealth of cultural treasures, including magnificent castles, charming medieval towns, and world-class museums.

German culture is renowned for its depth and richness, encompassing literature, music, art, philosophy, and cuisine. From the works of Goethe and Beethoven to the mouthwatering flavors of bratwurst and sauerkraut, Germany offers a feast for the senses that delights visitors from around the globe.

In this book, we will embark on a journey through the many facets of German life, exploring its history, geography, culture, and more. Whether you're planning a trip to Germany or simply seeking to deepen your understanding of this fascinating country, join me as we delve into everything you need to know about Germany.

Germany's Geographical Diversity: From Mountains to Coastlines

Germany's geographical diversity is nothing short of remarkable, offering a tapestry of landscapes that range from majestic mountains to picturesque coastlines. Situated in Central Europe, Germany shares borders with nine countries, including France, Switzerland, Austria, and Poland. This strategic location has not only shaped its history but also contributed to its rich natural heritage.

In the south, the Bavarian Alps dominate the landscape, with towering peaks, lush valleys, and crystal-clear lakes that beckon outdoor enthusiasts year-round. The highest mountain in Germany, the Zugspitze, rises to an impressive 2,962 meters (9,718 feet) above sea level and offers breathtaking views of the surrounding alpine scenery.

Moving northward, the terrain gradually gives way to rolling hills and verdant forests, characteristic of regions like the Black Forest and the Swabian Jura. These areas are not only renowned for their natural beauty but also for their cultural significance, with charming villages, ancient castles, and centuries-old traditions waiting to be discovered.

In the west, the Rhine River winds its way through the Rhine Valley, flanked by vineyards, medieval castles, and historic towns. The river serves as a vital waterway for transportation and trade, as well as a popular destination for river cruises and leisurely strolls along its scenic banks.

To the north, Germany's coastline stretches along the Baltic and North Seas, offering miles of sandy beaches, rugged cliffs, and windswept dunes. The islands of Sylt, Rügen, and Usedom are popular summer destinations, known for their pristine natural beauty and maritime charm.

Germany's central regions are characterized by fertile plains and river valleys, including the Elbe, Weser, and Main rivers, which crisscross the landscape and provide vital water resources for agriculture and industry.

Throughout the country, national parks and nature reserves protect and preserve Germany's natural heritage, providing habitats for a diverse array of plant and animal species. From the Bavarian Forest to the Wadden Sea, these protected areas offer opportunities for hiking, wildlife viewing, and immersive nature experiences.

In summary, Germany's geographical diversity is a testament to its rich natural heritage and cultural heritage, offering a wealth of landscapes to explore and enjoy. From the towering peaks of the Alps to the sandy shores of the North Sea, there's something for everyone to discover in this captivating country.

Early German History: From Ancient Tribes to Holy Roman Empire

Embark with me on a journey through the annals of early German history, a captivating saga that traces the origins of this land and its people from ancient tribes to the formation of the Holy Roman Empire. Our exploration begins millennia ago, in the prehistoric era, when various Germanic tribes inhabited the region we now know as Germany. These early inhabitants, including the Celts, Suebi, and Alemanni, lived in tribal societies, engaging in hunting, farming, and trade across the vast expanse of Central Europe.

As the Roman Empire expanded its reach into the region, encounters between Germanic tribes and Roman forces became more frequent. The Battle of the Teutoburg Forest in 9 AD, where Germanic warriors led by Arminius (also known as Hermann) ambushed and defeated three Roman legions, marked a significant turning point in the relationship between the Germanic peoples and the Roman Empire. The defeat halted Roman expansion into Germania and solidified the Germanic tribes' autonomy and independence.

In the centuries that followed, the Germanic tribes continued to evolve and interact with neighboring cultures, including the Franks, who established the Kingdom of the Franks in present-day France and Germany. Under the leadership of Charlemagne, also known as Charles the Great, the Franks expanded their territory and influence, forging alliances with Germanic tribes and consolidating power across Western Europe.

In 800 AD, Charlemagne was crowned Emperor of the Romans by Pope Leo III, marking the beginning of the Carolingian Empire and laying the foundation for the Holy Roman Empire. The Holy Roman Empire, which emerged in the 10th century, was a complex political entity that encompassed much of Central Europe, including parts of modern-day Germany, France, Italy, and beyond. It was characterized by a decentralized political structure, with power shared among the emperor, local princes, and ecclesiastical authorities.

Throughout the early medieval period, the Holy Roman Empire played a central role in shaping the political, social, and cultural landscape of Europe. It was a time of great upheaval and change, marked by conflicts between rival noble houses, religious schisms, and the spread of Christianity. The empire's influence extended far beyond its borders, as Germanic culture and language became dominant in much of Central Europe.

As we reflect on the early history of Germany, we are reminded of the resilience, ingenuity, and diversity of its people. From the ancient tribes who roamed the forests and plains to the emperors who ruled over vast domains, the story of early German history is one of ambition, struggle, and triumph. Join me as we continue our exploration of Germany's fascinating past, uncovering the layers of history that have shaped this remarkable land.

The Rise and Fall of Prussia: Shaping Modern Germany

Join me on a captivating journey through the rise and fall of Prussia, a pivotal chapter in the story of Germany's evolution into a modern nation-state. The history of Prussia is a tale of ambition, conquest, and cultural transformation that left an indelible mark on the landscape of Central Europe.

Prussia's origins can be traced back to the medieval Teutonic Order, a crusading military order tasked with converting and subjugating pagan tribes in the Baltic region. Over time, the Teutonic Knights established a powerful state known as the Monastic State of the Teutonic Knights, which later evolved into the Duchy of Prussia. In 1618, the Duchy of Prussia came under the rule of the Hohenzollern dynasty, marking the beginning of Prussia's rise to prominence.

Under the leadership of Frederick William, also known as the "Great Elector," Prussia began to assert itself as a formidable military and political power in Europe. Frederick William implemented a series of reforms that strengthened the state's economy, bureaucracy, and military, laying the groundwork for Prussia's future expansion and influence.

The zenith of Prussian power came during the reign of Frederick the Great, who ruled from 1740 to 1786. Frederick the Great was a skilled military strategist and statesman who expanded Prussia's territory through a series of successful wars and diplomatic maneuvers. His reign saw the acquisition of Silesia,

Pomerania, and other territories, solidifying Prussia's position as a major player in European affairs. Prussia's military prowess and administrative efficiency earned it a reputation as the "Sparta of the North" and a model for other European states to emulate. The Prussian army, disciplined and well-trained, became a symbol of national pride and unity, while Prussian bureaucracy set new standards for efficiency and governance. However, Prussia's fortunes began to wane in the 19th century, as it faced internal and external challenges that tested its resilience. The Napoleonic Wars and the Congress of Vienna reshaped the political map of Europe, leading to the dissolution of the Holy Roman Empire and the creation of the German Confederation, in which Prussia played a leading role.

In 1866, Prussia emerged victorious in the Austro-Prussian War, asserting its dominance over the other German states and laying the foundation for the unification of Germany under Prussian leadership. The following year, Otto von Bismarck, the "Iron Chancellor," orchestrated the creation of the North German Confederation, paving the way for the formation of the German Empire in 1871.

The unification of Germany marked the culmination of Prussia's quest for greatness, but it also sowed the seeds of its eventual downfall. The centralized nature of the German Empire marginalized the other German states and fueled tensions between Prussia and its neighbors, particularly France. These tensions erupted into the First World War, which ultimately led to the dissolution of the German Empire and the end of Prussian dominance in Europe.

World Wars and Their Impact on Germany

In the tumultuous history of Germany, the two World Wars stand as watershed moments that profoundly shaped the nation and its people. The First World War, which lasted from 1914 to 1918, brought about unprecedented destruction and loss of life. Germany, along with its allies, engaged in a brutal conflict against the Allied powers, facing off in a grueling war of attrition on multiple fronts. The war exacted a heavy toll on Germany, both in terms of human casualties and economic devastation.

Following Germany's defeat in the First World War, the Treaty of Versailles, signed in 1919, imposed harsh terms on the country, including significant territorial losses, demilitarization, and reparations payments. The treaty left a deep sense of resentment and humiliation among many Germans, fueling political instability and providing fertile ground for the rise of extremist ideologies.

The interwar period saw the emergence of the Weimar Republic, Germany's first experiment with democracy. However, the fledgling republic faced numerous challenges, including economic hardship, political polarization, and social unrest. In this volatile atmosphere, extremist movements, such as the Nazi Party led by Adolf Hitler, gained traction, promising to restore Germany's greatness and overturn the perceived injustices of the Versailles Treaty.

In 1933, Hitler was appointed Chancellor of Germany, marking the beginning of the Nazi regime's ascent to power. Under Hitler's leadership, Germany embarked on a path of aggressive expansionism and militarization, violating the terms of the Versailles Treaty and sparking international condemnation. The Second World War erupted in 1939, as Germany invaded Poland, triggering a global conflict that would engulf much of the world.

The Second World War proved even more catastrophic for Germany than the first, as the country faced defeat on multiple fronts and endured devastating bombing campaigns that laid waste to its cities and infrastructure. The Holocaust, perpetrated by the Nazi regime, resulted in the systematic genocide of six million Jews and millions of others deemed undesirable by the Nazis.

In 1945, Germany surrendered unconditionally, bringing an end to the war in Europe. The country lay in ruins, its cities reduced to rubble, and its population reeling from the horrors of war and genocide. Germany was divided into four occupation zones by the Allied powers, with the eastern portion falling under Soviet control and the western zones administered by the United States, Great Britain, and France.

The aftermath of the Second World War brought about profound changes in Germany's political and social landscape. The division of the country into East and West Germany, separated by the Iron Curtain, reflected the broader geopolitical tensions of the Cold War. In the West, the Federal Republic of Germany emerged as a democratic state, while in the East, the German Democratic Republic adopted a socialist system under Soviet influence.

The legacy of the World Wars continues to shape Germany's identity and national consciousness to this day. The country has reckoned with its past through acts of remembrance, reconciliation, and historical reflection, striving to confront the atrocities of the Nazi era and build a more peaceful and democratic future. The scars of war may fade, but the lessons learned from Germany's tumultuous history serve as a reminder of the enduring importance of vigilance, tolerance, and the pursuit of peace.

Post-War Germany: Division and Reunification

In the aftermath of the Second World War, Germany found itself divided both physically and ideologically. The country lay in ruins, its cities devastated by Allied bombing campaigns and its infrastructure in shambles. The victorious Allied powers, namely the United States, Soviet Union, Great Britain, and France, occupied Germany and set about establishing control over their respective zones of occupation.

The division of Germany into East and West was formalized in 1949 with the establishment of two separate states: the Federal Republic of Germany (West Germany) and the German Democratic Republic (East Germany). West Germany emerged as a democratic and capitalist state, aligned with the Western powers and integrated into the emerging framework of NATO and the European Economic Community. Meanwhile, East Germany adopted a socialist system under Soviet influence, with the ruling Socialist Unity Party (SED) tightly controlling political and economic life.

The division of Germany was symbolized by the construction of the Berlin Wall in 1961, which physically separated East and West Berlin and became a potent symbol of the Cold War division of Europe. The wall served as a stark reminder of the ideological and political divisions that defined the post-war era, as families were torn apart and communities divided by concrete and barbed wire.

Despite the geopolitical tensions and ideological differences, both East and West Germany experienced periods of economic growth and prosperity during the post-war years. West Germany, in particular, underwent a remarkable economic transformation, known as the "Wirtschaftswunder" or economic miracle, fueled by investment, innovation, and integration into the global economy. Meanwhile, East Germany struggled under the weight of a centrally planned economy and repressive political system, leading to widespread discontent and unrest among the population.

The division of Germany persisted for over four decades, with periodic tensions and crises threatening to escalate into open conflict. However, the winds of change began to blow in the late 1980s, as popular movements for reform and democracy gained momentum in Eastern Europe, culminating in the fall of the Berlin Wall on November 9, 1989.

The reunification of Germany, long considered an improbable dream, became a reality in 1990, as East and West Germany embarked on a path toward reconciliation and integration. On October 3, 1990, the two German states formally reunited to form a single, sovereign nation, marking the end of the Cold War division of Europe and the beginning of a new era of German unity.

The reunification process was complex and challenging, as East Germany struggled to adapt to the economic and political realities of a unified Germany. The integration of East German institutions, industries, and infrastructure into the broader German framework required significant investment and restructuring, leading to economic disparities and social tensions that persist to this day.

Despite the challenges, reunification represented a triumph of hope over division, as Germans on both sides of the former border embraced the opportunity to build a shared future based on democracy, freedom, and prosperity. The reunified Germany emerged as a leading economic and political power in Europe, playing a central role in shaping the continent's future and advancing the cause of peace and reconciliation on the world stage.

Contemporary German Politics and Government

Let's delve into the intricacies of contemporary German politics and government, where the principles of democracy and federalism guide the nation's governance. At the helm is the Federal Republic of Germany, a parliamentary democracy comprised of 16 federal states, each with its own government and legislature. The federal government, based in Berlin, operates within a framework established by the Basic Law, Germany's constitution adopted in 1949.

The political landscape of Germany is characterized by a multi-party system, with a variety of parties vying for representation in the Bundestag, the lower house of the federal parliament. The two largest parties historically have been the center-right Christian Democratic Union (CDU) and its Bavarian sister party, the Christian Social Union (CSU), and the center-left Social Democratic Party (SPD). Other significant parties include the Green Party, the Free Democratic Party (FDP), and the Left Party.

Germany's head of state is the Federal President, a largely ceremonial role whose duties include representing the country domestically and internationally. The Federal President is elected by a special assembly composed of members of the Bundestag and representatives from the federal states. The Chancellor, on the other hand, serves as the head of government and is responsible for overseeing the executive branch. The Chancellor is typically the leader of the majority party in the Bundestag and is appointed by the Federal President.

The Bundestag plays a central role in German politics, serving as the primary legislative body responsible for passing laws, approving the federal budget, and overseeing the government's activities. Members of the Bundestag are elected through a system of mixed-member proportional representation, which combines direct elections with proportional representation to ensure fair and representative outcomes.

In addition to the Bundestag, Germany also has the Bundesrat, the upper house of the federal parliament, which represents the interests of the federal states. The Bundesrat consists of representatives from the governments of the federal states and has the power to veto legislation that affects their interests.

Germany's political system is known for its stability and consensus-oriented approach to governance, with coalitions often formed between multiple parties to achieve majority support for legislation. This system of coalition government fosters compromise and cooperation among political parties, contributing to Germany's reputation as a model of effective governance.

In recent years, Germany has faced a range of political challenges, including debates over immigration, climate change, and the role of Germany in the European Union. The rise of populist and far-right movements has also added a new dimension to the political landscape, challenging traditional party structures and norms.

Despite these challenges, Germany remains committed to the principles of democracy, rule of law, and human rights, serving as a beacon of stability and prosperity in a rapidly changing world.

German Economy: Engineering Powerhouse and Global Player

Let's dive into the fascinating world of the German economy, a powerhouse of innovation, efficiency, and global influence. Germany's economic success story is built on a foundation of engineering excellence, manufacturing prowess, and a strong tradition of craftsmanship. Known for its precision engineering and high-quality manufacturing, Germany has earned a reputation as a world leader in industries such as automotive, machinery, and electronics.

The German economy is the largest in Europe and the fourth-largest in the world by nominal GDP, boasting a highly developed industrial base and a skilled workforce. With a focus on research and development, Germany has fostered a culture of innovation that drives technological advancements and fuels economic growth. German companies are at the forefront of cutting-edge industries such as renewable energy, biotechnology, and information technology, contributing to the country's status as a global innovation hub.

One of Germany's key economic strengths lies in its Mittelstand, a network of small and medium-sized enterprises (SMEs) that form the backbone of the economy. These family-owned businesses are known for their specialization, flexibility, and commitment to quality, allowing them to compete successfully in niche markets around the world. The

Mittelstand plays a crucial role in driving innovation, creating jobs, and sustaining economic growth across Germany.

Germany's export-oriented economy is another hallmark of its success, with exports accounting for a significant portion of its GDP. The country is a leading exporter of automobiles, machinery, chemicals, and pharmaceuticals, with key trading partners including the United States, China, and European Union countries. Germany's export-driven model has helped to maintain a strong trade surplus, bolstering its economic stability and competitiveness on the global stage.

The automotive industry is a cornerstone of the German economy, with iconic brands such as Volkswagen, BMW, and Mercedes-Benz synonymous with quality, performance, and innovation. Germany is the world's third-largest producer of automobiles, producing millions of vehicles annually and exporting them to markets around the world. The automotive sector also supports a vast ecosystem of suppliers, manufacturers, and service providers, generating employment and economic activity across the country.

In addition to manufacturing, Germany's services sector is also a significant contributor to the economy, encompassing areas such as finance, healthcare, tourism, and logistics. Frankfurt, Germany's financial capital, is home to the European Central Bank and serves as a major financial hub, while cities like Munich and Berlin are renowned for their vibrant startup scenes and entrepreneurial spirit.

Germany's economic success is underpinned by a strong commitment to education, vocational training, and lifelong learning. The country's dual education system, which combines classroom instruction with on-the-job training, produces a skilled workforce that is highly sought after by employers around the world. Germany's emphasis on technical education and apprenticeships ensures that its workforce remains adaptable, innovative, and competitive in the global marketplace.

German Education System: Excellence and Efficiency

Let's explore the German education system, renowned for its emphasis on excellence, efficiency, and lifelong learning. From early childhood education to vocational training and higher education, Germany offers a comprehensive and inclusive approach to learning that prepares students for success in a rapidly changing world.

At the heart of the German education system is the principle of equality of opportunity, ensuring that every child has access to high-quality education regardless of their background or socioeconomic status. Education is compulsory for children between the ages of six and 15, with most students attending primary school for four years followed by secondary education.

Germany's education system is decentralized, with each of the 16 federal states responsible for setting its own educational policies and curriculum standards. This diversity allows for flexibility and innovation while maintaining a commitment to national standards and quality assurance.

Early childhood education plays a crucial role in laying the foundation for lifelong learning and development. Germany offers a range of early childhood education and care options, including daycare centers, kindergartens, and preschools, that focus on nurturing children's social, emotional, and cognitive skills in a supportive and stimulating environment.

Primary education in Germany typically begins at age six and lasts for four years, culminating in the Grundschule, or primary school. The curriculum emphasizes core subjects such as mathematics, science, language arts, and social studies, as well as extracurricular activities, sports, and arts education.

After completing primary school, students move on to secondary education, where they are placed into one of several different tracks based on their academic abilities and career aspirations. The three main types of secondary schools in Germany are the Gymnasium, which prepares students for university entrance; the Realschule, which offers a more practical and vocational-oriented curriculum; and the Hauptschule, which focuses on basic skills and prepares students for vocational training or entry-level employment.

One of the unique features of the German education system is its dual education system, which combines classroom instruction with on-the-job training in a wide range of skilled trades and professions. Apprenticeships typically last between two and three years and provide students with hands-on experience, industry-recognized qualifications, and a pathway to employment.

Higher education in Germany is highly regarded worldwide, with its universities consistently ranked among the best in the world. Germany offers a wide range of undergraduate and graduate programs, including traditional academic disciplines, applied sciences, and professional fields such as engineering, medicine, and business.

One of the most distinctive aspects of higher education in Germany is its commitment to affordability and accessibility. Public universities in Germany do not charge tuition fees for undergraduate programs, making higher education accessible to students from all walks of life. Additionally, Germany offers a range of scholarships, grants, and financial aid programs to support students throughout their academic journey.

Overall, the German education system reflects a deep commitment to excellence, innovation, and lifelong learning. By providing students with a solid foundation in core academic subjects, hands-on practical experience, and opportunities for personal and professional growth, Germany prepares its citizens to thrive in a rapidly changing global economy and society.

German Language: A Key to Understanding Culture and Society

Let's delve into the intricate world of the German language, a linguistic treasure trove that offers insight into the culture, history, and society of Germany. With over 100 million speakers worldwide, German is one of the most widely spoken languages in Europe and serves as the official language of Germany, Austria, and Liechtenstein, as well as being one of the official languages of Switzerland, Luxembourg, and Belgium.

German is a Germanic language, belonging to the same linguistic family as English, Dutch, and Swedish. It shares many similarities with these languages, including grammatical structures, vocabulary, and phonetics, making it relatively accessible for English speakers to learn.

One of the distinctive features of the German language is its complex system of noun declensions, verb conjugations, and grammatical cases. German nouns are assigned one of four grammatical cases (nominative, accusative, dative, and genitive), which dictate their role in a sentence and determine the form of accompanying articles, adjectives, and pronouns. While this aspect of German grammar can be challenging for learners, mastering it opens up a world of expressive possibilities and precision in communication.

German is also known for its extensive vocabulary, with a rich assortment of words and expressions that reflect the country's cultural heritage, technological prowess, and philosophical tradition. From compound nouns like "Schadenfreude" (taking pleasure in someone else's misfortune) to philosophical concepts like "Weltschmerz" (world-weariness), German offers nuanced ways of articulating thoughts, feelings, and experiences.

In addition to its literary and philosophical contributions, the German language is also a key to understanding Germany's vibrant cultural landscape. German literature has a rich tradition dating back to the Middle Ages, with towering figures such as Johann Wolfgang von Goethe, Friedrich Schiller, and Thomas Mann leaving an indelible mark on world literature. German poetry, drama, and prose have explored themes ranging from romanticism and existentialism to political activism and social critique, providing insight into the complexities of the human experience.

Furthermore, the German language is closely intertwined with Germany's musical heritage, with composers such as Ludwig van Beethoven, Wolfgang Amadeus Mozart, and Johann Sebastian Bach creating timeless masterpieces that continue to captivate audiences around the world. Whether it's the stirring symphonies of Beethoven or the delicate melodies of Schubert's lieder, German music offers a window into the country's soul and psyche.

Beyond literature and music, the German language also plays a central role in shaping the country's social and political discourse. Germany has a strong tradition of public debate and intellectual inquiry, with newspapers, magazines, and online forums serving as platforms for dialogue and exchange. Understanding German allows one to engage directly with these conversations, gaining insight into current events, social issues, and political debates.

In conclusion, the German language is far more than just a means of communication; it is a gateway to understanding the culture, history, and society of Germany. By delving into its grammar, vocabulary, literature, music, and public discourse, one gains a deeper appreciation for the rich tapestry of German culture and the complexities of the human experience.

Exploring German Wildlife: From the Black Forest to the Baltic Sea

Let's embark on an adventure through the diverse and captivating wildlife of Germany, where lush forests, rolling hills, and pristine coastlines provide habitats for a wide array of plant and animal species. From the ancient woodlands of the Black Forest to the windswept shores of the Baltic Sea, Germany's natural landscapes teem with life, offering opportunities for exploration, discovery, and conservation.

The Black Forest, nestled in the southwest corner of Germany, is one of the country's most iconic natural landmarks. Covering an area of over 4,000 square miles, this ancient forest is home to a rich diversity of flora and fauna, including towering spruce and fir trees, elusive lynx and red deer, and vibrant bird species such as the black woodpecker and European nightjar. Visitors to the Black Forest can explore its network of hiking trails, scenic viewpoints, and charming villages, immersing themselves in the beauty and tranquility of this enchanting wilderness.

As we journey eastward, we encounter the Bavarian Alps, a majestic mountain range that stretches along the southern border of Germany. Here, alpine meadows, rugged peaks, and crystal-clear lakes provide habitat for a variety of alpine species, including chamois, ibex, and golden eagles. The Bavarian Alps are also home to iconic wildlife such as the Alpine marmot, a social and industrious rodent known for its distinctive whistle and burrowing behavior. Venturing northward, we reach the Baltic Sea, where coastal dunes, salt marshes, and sandy beaches support a rich mosaic of marine and terrestrial life. The Baltic Sea is a vital habitat for migratory birds, including terns, gulls, and waders, which flock to its shores to breed and feed during the summer months. Seals, porpoises, and other marine mammals can also be spotted offshore, while coastal forests provide refuge for roe deer, wild boar, and European hares.

Inland, Germany's river systems, including the Rhine, Danube, and Elbe, are lifelines for a wide variety of aquatic species, including fish, amphibians, and invertebrates. The Rhine River, in particular, is renowned for its biodiversity, supporting populations of salmon, sturgeon, and freshwater mussels, as well as providing habitat for otters and beavers along its banks.

Throughout Germany, national parks, nature reserves, and protected areas safeguard and preserve the country's natural heritage, ensuring that future generations can continue to enjoy and appreciate its beauty and diversity. From the Harz Mountains to the Spreewald Biosphere Reserve, these protected areas offer opportunities for outdoor recreation, wildlife viewing, and environmental education, serving as invaluable resources for conservation and stewardship.

As we conclude our exploration of German wildlife, we are reminded of the importance of preserving and protecting the natural world for future generations. By embracing sustainable practices, supporting conservation efforts, and fostering a deeper connection with nature, we can ensure that Germany's rich biodiversity continues to thrive for years to come.

Savory Delights: A Culinary Journey Through German Cuisine

Join me on a mouthwatering journey through the flavors and traditions of German cuisine, where hearty dishes, savory meats, and delectable pastries await at every turn. German cuisine is deeply rooted in regional ingredients, culinary techniques, and cultural influences, reflecting the country's diverse landscape and rich history.

Let's start with the classics. No exploration of German cuisine would be complete without mentioning sausages, or "wurst" in German. From bratwurst to currywurst, Germany boasts a wide variety of sausage specialties, each with its own unique flavor profile and regional variations. Served hot off the grill or simmered in a hearty stew, sausages are a staple of German cuisine and a beloved comfort food for locals and visitors alike.

Accompanying these savory delights are an assortment of side dishes and accompaniments that add depth and flavor to any meal. Sauerkraut, a fermented cabbage dish, is a ubiquitous accompaniment to sausages and other meat dishes, providing a tangy and slightly sour contrast to rich and savory flavors. Potato dishes also feature prominently in German cuisine, with favorites such as potato salad, potato dumplings, and crispy potato pancakes known as "kartoffelpuffer" or "reiberdatschi."

Moving on to main courses, German cuisine offers a hearty array of meat dishes that are sure to satisfy even the heartiest of appetites. Schnitzel, a breaded and fried cutlet usually made from pork or veal, is a classic favorite that can be found on menus across the country. Served with a squeeze of lemon and a side of potato salad or fries, schnitzel is a quintessential German comfort food.

Another beloved meat dish is "schweinshaxe," or roasted pork knuckle, a hearty and flavorful dish that is often served with sauerkraut and potato dumplings. The crispy skin and tender meat of the pork knuckle make it a favorite at beer gardens and traditional taverns throughout Germany.

For those with a sweet tooth, German cuisine offers a delightful array of pastries, cakes, and desserts that are sure to tantalize the taste buds. Black Forest cake, made with layers of chocolate sponge cake, cherries, and whipped cream, is perhaps one of the most famous German desserts, known for its rich and indulgent flavors. Apple strudel, a flaky pastry filled with spiced apples, raisins, and nuts, is another beloved classic that pairs perfectly with a dollop of vanilla ice cream or whipped cream.

To wash it all down, Germany is famous for its beer, which is brewed according to centuries-old traditions and purity laws. With over 1,300 breweries producing a staggering variety of beer styles, from crisp lagers to rich and malty bocks, Germany is a beer lover's paradise. Whether enjoyed at a bustling beer hall in Munich or a cozy tavern in the countryside, German beer is an integral part of the country's culinary heritage and a testament to its brewing expertise.

As we conclude our culinary journey through German cuisine, we are left with a newfound appreciation for the rich flavors, hearty dishes, and time-honored traditions that define this vibrant culinary landscape. From savory sausages to decadent pastries, German cuisine offers something for every palate and occasion, inviting us to savor each bite and savor the rich tapestry of flavors that make it truly unique.

Berlin: Germany's Vibrant Capital and Historical Center

Situated in the northeastern part of the country, Berlin is not only the largest city in Germany but also one of Europe's most influential and cosmopolitan metropolises.

Berlin's rich history stretches back over 800 years, with its origins dating to the 13th century when it was founded as a trading hub on the banks of the Spree River. Over the centuries, Berlin grew into a thriving center of commerce, culture, and political power, serving as the capital of the Kingdom of Prussia, the German Empire, the Weimar Republic, and ultimately, modern-day Germany.

The city's tumultuous history is reflected in its architecture, with a mix of medieval landmarks, grand palaces, Soviet-era buildings, and sleek modern structures dotting the skyline. One of Berlin's most iconic landmarks is the Brandenburg Gate, a neoclassical triumphal arch that has come to symbolize the city's unity and resilience. Nearby, the Reichstag building, home to the German parliament, is a testament to Berlin's democratic ideals and commitment to openness and transparency.

Berlin is also known for its vibrant arts and cultural scene, with world-class museums, galleries, theaters, and concert halls showcasing a diverse array of artistic expression. The Museum Island, a UNESCO World Heritage site located in the heart of the city, is home to a cluster of museums and cultural institutions, including the Pergamon Museum, the Altes Museum, and the Neues Museum, which house priceless collections of art, artifacts, and archaeological treasures from around the world.

In addition to its cultural attractions, Berlin is a mecca for music lovers, with a thriving nightlife scene that encompasses everything from underground clubs and electronic music festivals to classical concerts and opera performances. The city's diverse population and reputation for tolerance and inclusivity make it a magnet for artists, musicians, and creatives from around the globe, who flock to Berlin to seek inspiration and opportunity.

Berlin's neighborhoods are as diverse as its inhabitants, each offering its own unique blend of history, culture, and charm. From the bohemian vibe of Kreuzberg and the hipster haven of Friedrichshain to the upscale elegance of Charlottenburg and the leafy tranquility of Prenzlauer Berg, Berlin's neighborhoods reflect the city's dynamic and ever-evolving character.

Despite its turbulent past, Berlin has emerged as a beacon of hope, progress, and reconciliation in the 21st century. The fall of the Berlin Wall in 1989 symbolized the end of division and the beginning of a new era of unity and freedom for the city and its people. Today, Berlin stands as a testament to the power of resilience, reinvention, and the human spirit, inviting visitors to explore its streets, discover its stories, and experience the magic of this remarkable city firsthand.

Munich: Bavaria's Heartbeat and Oktoberfest Hub

Nestled in the heart of southern Germany, Munich is known for its rich history, stunning architecture, and lively atmosphere.

At the center of Munich's cultural scene is its celebrated beer culture, embodied by the world-famous Oktoberfest. Held annually in late September to early October, Oktoberfest is the world's largest beer festival, attracting millions of visitors from around the globe to Munich's Theresienwiese fairgrounds. Here, revelers indulge in traditional Bavarian beer, hearty food, and live music, all amidst the festive atmosphere of colorful tents and carnival rides.

But Munich's beer culture extends far beyond Oktoberfest. The city is home to a wealth of historic beer halls, breweries, and beer gardens, where locals and visitors alike gather to enjoy a cold brew and soak up the Bavarian ambiance. Favorites include the legendary Hofbräuhaus, a centuries-old beer hall that epitomizes Munich's beer culture with its lively atmosphere, hearty cuisine, and traditional Bavarian music.

Beyond its beer scene, Munich boasts a rich cultural heritage that is reflected in its architecture, museums, and landmarks. The city's historic center, known as the Altstadt, is a treasure trove of architectural gems, including the majestic

Frauenkirche, the imposing Neues Rathaus (New Town Hall), and the opulent Residenz palace, former seat of the Bavarian monarchs.

Munich is also renowned for its world-class museums and galleries, which showcase a diverse range of art, history, and culture. The Alte Pinakothek houses one of the most important collections of Old Master paintings in the world, while the Deutsches Museum offers a fascinating journey through the history of science and technology. Other notable museums include the Lenbachhaus, home to an impressive collection of modern art, and the BMW Museum, which celebrates the history and innovation of the iconic German automaker.

In addition to its cultural attractions, Munich is a city of green spaces and outdoor recreation. The Englischer Garten, one of the largest urban parks in the world, offers miles of walking and biking trails, scenic picnic spots, and even a surf wave on the Eisbach river. The city's numerous beer gardens, nestled amidst lush foliage and shaded by chestnut trees, provide the perfect setting for relaxation and socializing on a sunny afternoon.

Munich's culinary scene is equally impressive, with a diverse array of restaurants, cafes, and food markets serving up delicious Bavarian specialties and international cuisine. From traditional dishes like weißwurst (white sausage) with sweet mustard and pretzels to innovative gourmet creations,

Munich offers something to satisfy every palate and craving.

As the cultural, economic, and social heart of Bavaria, Munich embodies the spirit of tradition, innovation, and joie de vivre that defines this vibrant region of Germany. Whether you're exploring its historic landmarks, sampling its world-class beer, or simply soaking up its lively atmosphere, Munich is sure to leave a lasting impression on visitors and locals alike.

Hamburg: Port City Splendor and Maritime Heritage

Welcome to Hamburg, a city of port city splendor and rich maritime heritage nestled along the banks of the Elbe River in northern Germany. As one of Europe's largest ports and a key hub of international trade, Hamburg has long been a gateway to the world, welcoming ships, goods, and people from across the globe.

At the heart of Hamburg's maritime identity is its bustling port, one of the busiest and most important in Europe. Stretching along the shores of the Elbe River and encompassing a network of docks, terminals, and warehouses, the Port of Hamburg handles millions of tons of cargo each year, including containers, bulk goods, and cruise ships. The port's iconic cranes and industrial skyline are a testament to Hamburg's role as a center of global commerce and maritime activity.

Beyond its port, Hamburg is also known for its picturesque waterways, including the Alster Lakes and the canals of the Speicherstadt, or Warehouse District. Built in the late 19th and early 20th centuries, the Speicherstadt is a UNESCO World Heritage site and one of Hamburg's most iconic landmarks, with its red-brick warehouses, cobbled streets, and charming bridges creating a picturesque backdrop for leisurely strolls and boat tours.

Hamburg's maritime heritage is also evident in its cultural institutions and attractions. The International Maritime Museum, located in a historic warehouse in the Speicherstadt, houses one of the world's largest collections of maritime artifacts, including ship models, navigational instruments, and historical documents. Nearby, the Rickmer Rickmers, a historic sailing ship turned museum, offers visitors the chance to explore life aboard a 19th-century tall ship.

In addition to its maritime attractions, Hamburg is a city of vibrant neighborhoods, diverse culture, and thriving arts scene. The lively district of St. Pauli is home to the famous Reeperbahn, a bustling entertainment strip known for its bars, clubs, and theaters. Nearby, the HafenCity neighborhood is undergoing a transformation into a modern waterfront district, with sleek architecture, trendy cafes, and cultural landmarks such as the Elbphilharmonie concert hall.

Hamburg's culinary scene is as diverse as its neighborhoods, with a wide range of restaurants, cafes, and street food stalls serving up delicious regional specialties and international cuisine. From fresh seafood and traditional German dishes like Labskaus (a hearty sailor's stew) to innovative fusion cuisine and gourmet dining experiences, Hamburg offers something to satisfy every palate and culinary craving.

As a city of port city splendor and maritime heritage, Hamburg invites visitors to explore its rich history, vibrant culture, and dynamic waterfront. Whether you're admiring the view from the Elbphilharmonie, strolling along the banks of the Alster Lakes, or sampling fresh fish at the Fischmarkt, Hamburg offers a memorable experience that is sure to leave a lasting impression.

Frankfurt: Financial Hub and Modern Skyline

Situated in the heart of the country, Frankfurt is not only the largest city in the state of Hesse but also a global center for finance, commerce, and innovation.

At the center of Frankfurt's skyline stands the iconic Main Tower, a symbol of the city's modernity and economic prowess. Rising 200 meters above the city streets, the Main Tower offers panoramic views of Frankfurt and its surrounding landscape, showcasing the city's gleaming skyscrapers, historic landmarks, and lush green spaces.

Frankfurt's role as a financial hub dates back centuries, with the city's origins as a trading center along the banks of the Main River. Today, Frankfurt is home to the European Central Bank, the Deutsche Bundesbank, and the Frankfurt Stock Exchange, making it one of the world's leading financial centers. The city's financial district, known as the Bankenviertel, is characterized by its towering office buildings, bustling streets, and vibrant atmosphere, with bankers, traders, and business professionals from around the world converging on Frankfurt to conduct business and make deals.

But Frankfurt is more than just a center of finance; it is also a city of culture, history, and diversity. The historic district of Altstadt, or Old Town, is home to charming cobblestone streets, medieval churches, and half-timbered houses, offering a glimpse into

Frankfurt's rich past. Nearby, the Römerberg square is a popular gathering spot, with its picturesque buildings and lively atmosphere making it a favorite destination for tourists and locals alike.

Frankfurt's cultural scene is also thriving, with world-class museums, galleries, and theaters showcasing a diverse array of art, history, and performance. The Städel Museum, one of Germany's most important art museums, houses a vast collection of European masterpieces spanning centuries, while the Schirn Kunsthalle showcases contemporary art from around the world. The Alte Oper, a grand concert hall dating back to the 19th century, hosts classical music concerts, opera performances, and other cultural events throughout the year.

In addition to its cultural attractions, Frankfurt is a city of green spaces and outdoor recreation. The Palmengarten, one of Europe's largest botanical gardens, offers a tranquil oasis amidst the urban hustle and bustle, with colorful flowerbeds, exotic plants, and peaceful walking paths. The nearby Frankfurt City Forest provides opportunities for hiking, cycling, and picnicking, allowing residents and visitors to escape the city and connect with nature.

Frankfurt's culinary scene is equally diverse, with a wide range of restaurants, cafes, and food markets serving up delicious regional specialties and international cuisine. From traditional German dishes like Apfelwein (apple wine) and Grüne Soße (green sauce) to global flavors from around the world, Frankfurt offers something to satisfy every palate and culinary craving.

As a city of financial hub and modern skyline, Frankfurt invites visitors to explore its rich history, vibrant culture, and dynamic urban landscape. Whether you're admiring the view from the Main Tower, exploring the museums of Museumsufer, or savoring the flavors of local cuisine, Frankfurt offers a memorable experience that is sure to leave a lasting impression.

Cologne: Gothic Splendor and Rhine River Charm

Welcome to Cologne, a city of gothic splendor and Rhine River charm, nestled in the western part of Germany. With its rich history, stunning architecture, and picturesque riverside setting, Cologne is a destination that captivates visitors from around the world.

At the heart of Cologne's skyline stands the magnificent Cologne Cathedral, or Kölner Dom, a UNESCO World Heritage site and one of the most iconic landmarks in Germany. Towering over the city at 157 meters tall, the cathedral's twin spires dominate the skyline and serve as a symbol of Cologne's enduring spiritual and architectural legacy. Built over the course of six centuries, the Cologne Cathedral is a masterpiece of gothic architecture, with its intricate stone carvings, stained glass windows, and soaring vaulted ceilings drawing millions of visitors each year.

Beyond the cathedral, Cologne is home to a wealth of historic landmarks, charming neighborhoods, and cultural attractions. The Old Town, or Altstadt, is a maze of narrow cobblestone streets, medieval squares, and quaint shops and cafes, offering a glimpse into Cologne's rich past. The Alter Markt, or Old Market Square, is a focal point of the Altstadt, with its colorful buildings and bustling atmosphere making it a favorite gathering spot for locals and tourists alike.

Cologne's cultural scene is also vibrant and diverse, with museums, galleries, and theaters showcasing a wide range of art, history, and performance. The Museum Ludwig is one of Germany's most important modern art museums, with its extensive collection of works by Picasso, Warhol, and other contemporary artists. The Romano-Germanic Museum offers insight into Cologne's Roman past, with artifacts and exhibits exploring the city's ancient history.

One of Cologne's most beloved traditions is its annual Carnival celebration, a lively and festive event that takes place in the weeks leading up to Lent. Known locally as "Karneval," Carnival is a time of colorful parades, elaborate costumes, and raucous street parties, with locals and visitors alike joining in the revelry and merriment. The highlight of the Carnival season is Rosenmontag, or Rose Monday, when elaborate floats parade through the streets of Cologne, accompanied by music, dancing, and laughter.

Cologne's location along the Rhine River adds to its charm and allure, with scenic river cruises, waterfront promenades, and picturesque bridges offering stunning views of the city and surrounding countryside. The Rhine River is also a vital transportation artery, connecting Cologne to other cities and regions along its banks and serving as a lifeline for trade and commerce throughout the centuries.

In addition to its cultural and historical attractions, Cologne is a city of culinary delights, with a wide range of restaurants, breweries, and food markets serving up delicious regional specialties and international cuisine. From hearty German dishes like kölsch (local beer) and kölsche kaviar (blood sausage) to global flavors from around the world, Cologne offers something to satisfy every palate and culinary craving.

As a city of gothic splendor and Rhine River charm, Cologne invites visitors to explore its rich history, vibrant culture, and picturesque surroundings. Whether you're admiring the soaring spires of the Cologne Cathedral, strolling along the banks of the Rhine, or sampling the flavors of local cuisine, Cologne offers a memorable experience that is sure to leave a lasting impression.

Heidelberg: Romanticism and Scholarly Legacy

Renowned for its romantic charm, historic architecture, and scholarly legacy, Heidelberg is a destination that enchants visitors with its beauty and intellectual vibrancy.

At the heart of Heidelberg's allure is its stunning Old Town, or Altstadt, a maze of narrow cobblestone streets, medieval buildings, and quaint squares that exude old-world charm. The centerpiece of the Old Town is the majestic Heidelberg Castle, or Schloss Heidelberg, perched atop a hill overlooking the city. Dating back to the 13th century, the castle is a symbol of Heidelberg's rich history and architectural grandeur, with its crumbling ruins and panoramic views attracting visitors from around the world.

Heidelberg is also renowned for its prestigious university, the Ruprecht-Karls-Universität Heidelberg, one of the oldest and most renowned universities in Europe. Founded in 1386, the university has a long tradition of academic excellence and intellectual inquiry, with notable alumni including philosophers such as Georg Wilhelm Friedrich Hegel and Max Weber, and scientists such as Robert Bunsen and Hermann von Helmholtz. Today, the university continues to attract students and scholars from around the world, contributing to Heidelberg's reputation as a center of learning and innovation.

In addition to its castle and university, Heidelberg is known for its romantic ambiance, which has inspired poets, writers, and artists for centuries. The city's picturesque riverside promenades, lush green parks, and charming cafes create an idyllic setting for leisurely strolls and romantic encounters. The Philosophenweg, or Philosopher's Walk, offers stunning views of the Old Town and Neckar River, providing the perfect backdrop for contemplation and reflection.

Heidelberg's cultural scene is also vibrant, with theaters, galleries, and music venues showcasing a diverse array of artistic expression. The Heidelberger Frühling, or Heidelberg Spring, is an annual music festival that attracts world-class musicians and ensembles to perform in venues throughout the city. The Heidelberger Schlossfestspiele, or Heidelberg Castle Festival, is a summer theater festival that brings classical and contemporary plays to the castle's historic courtyard, enchanting audiences with its magical ambiance and dramatic performances.

Heidelberg's culinary scene is equally enticing, with a variety of restaurants, wine bars, and beer gardens offering delicious regional specialties and international cuisine. The city is known for its hearty German dishes such as schnitzel, bratwurst, and käsespätzle (cheese noodles), as well as its fine wines from the nearby vineyards of the Rhine and Neckar valleys.

As a city of romanticism and scholarly legacy, Heidelberg invites visitors to immerse themselves in its rich history, intellectual atmosphere, and natural beauty. Whether you're exploring the ruins of the castle, attending a lecture at the university, or simply enjoying a leisurely stroll along the river, Heidelberg offers a memorable experience that captures the imagination and leaves a lasting impression.

Dresden: Baroque Beauty Rising from the Ashes

Situated on the banks of the Elbe River in eastern Germany, Dresden is known for its stunning architecture, rich cultural heritage, and remarkable resilience in the face of adversity.

At the heart of Dresden's architectural splendor is the historic Altstadt, or Old Town, a UNESCO World Heritage site that boasts a wealth of baroque and rococo masterpieces. The Frauenkirche, or Church of Our Lady, is perhaps the most iconic landmark in Dresden, with its towering dome and elegant facade dominating the city skyline. Originally built in the 18th century, the Frauenkirche was destroyed during the bombing of Dresden in World War II and meticulously reconstructed in the decades following the war, symbolizing the city's resilience and determination to rebuild.

Nearby, the Zwinger Palace is another architectural gem that showcases Dresden's baroque grandeur. Designed by court architect Matthäus Daniel Pöppelmann in the early 18th century, the Zwinger is a stunning example of baroque architecture, with its ornate pavilions, fountains, and galleries creating a picturesque backdrop for cultural events and exhibitions. Today, the Zwinger houses several museums and collections, including the Old Masters Picture Gallery, which features works by artists such as Raphael, Rembrandt, and Vermeer. Dresden's cultural scene is also enriched by its numerous museums, galleries, and theaters, which offer a diverse array of art, history, and performance. The Dresden

State Art Collections comprise a network of museums and institutions that house some of Europe's most important collections of art and artifacts, including the Albertinum, the Dresden Castle, and the Grünes Gewölbe, or Green Vault, a treasure trove of priceless jewels, precious metals, and decorative objects.

In addition to its cultural attractions, Dresden is known for its natural beauty and scenic landscapes. The Elbe River, which winds its way through the city, provides opportunities for leisurely boat cruises, riverside picnics, and scenic walks along its picturesque banks. The nearby Saxon Switzerland National Park offers breathtaking vistas of sandstone cliffs, lush forests, and meandering rivers, providing outdoor enthusiasts with endless opportunities for hiking, climbing, and exploration.

Dresden's culinary scene is a reflection of its rich cultural heritage, with a variety of restaurants, cafes, and beer gardens serving up delicious regional specialties and international cuisine. From hearty Saxon dishes like Sauerbraten (pot roast) and Dresdner Stollen (fruitcake) to gourmet dining experiences and trendy street food markets, Dresden offers something to satisfy every palate and culinary craving.

As a city of baroque beauty rising from the ashes, Dresden invites visitors to explore its rich history, vibrant culture, and stunning architecture. Whether you're admiring the skyline from the banks of the Elbe, exploring the galleries of the Zwinger Palace, or savoring the flavors of local cuisine, Dresden offers a memorable experience that celebrates its resilience, creativity, and enduring spirit.

Leipzig: Music, Literature, and Cultural Crossroads

Leipzig's rich history and vibrant arts scene have earned it a reputation as a cultural capital, attracting artists, musicians, and intellectuals from around the world.

At the heart of Leipzig's cultural legacy is its illustrious musical heritage. The city is perhaps best known as the hometown of Johann Sebastian Bach, one of the greatest composers in history. Bach spent the majority of his career in Leipzig, serving as the music director at the St. Thomas Church and School from 1723 until his death in 1750. Today, Leipzig pays tribute to its musical prodigy with the annual Bachfest, a celebration of his life and work that attracts music lovers and performers from far and wide.

But Leipzig's musical legacy extends far beyond Bach. The city also played a crucial role in the development of classical music during the 19th century, serving as a hub for composers such as Felix Mendelssohn and Robert Schumann. Mendelssohn, in particular, had a profound influence on Leipzig's musical scene, serving as the conductor of the Leipzig Gewandhaus Orchestra and establishing the Leipzig Conservatory, which would later become the University of Music and Theatre Leipzig.

In addition to its musical heritage, Leipzig is also known for its literary tradition, with a long list of writers, poets, and thinkers who have called the city home. The Leipzig Book Fair, one of the oldest and largest book fairs in Europe, has been held annually since the 17th century, attracting authors, publishers, and book lovers from around the world. Leipzig's literary scene is further enriched by its numerous bookstores, publishing houses, and literary cafes, which provide spaces for writers and readers to connect and share ideas.

Leipzig's cultural crossroads are evident in its diverse population and vibrant arts scene, which encompasses theater, dance, visual arts, and more. The city's creative energy can be felt in its lively neighborhoods, historic landmarks, and modern cultural institutions. The Spinnerei, a former cotton mill turned art complex, is now home to dozens of galleries, studios, and exhibition spaces, showcasing the work of emerging and established artists from Leipzig and beyond.

In addition to its cultural attractions, Leipzig is a city of green spaces and outdoor recreation, with parks, gardens, and nature reserves providing opportunities for relaxation and leisure. The Leipzig Zoo, one of the oldest in the world, is home to thousands of animals from around the globe, making it a popular destination for families and nature enthusiasts alike.

Leipzig's culinary scene reflects its diverse cultural influences, with a variety of restaurants, cafes, and street food stalls serving up delicious regional specialties and international cuisine. From hearty Saxon dishes like Leipziger Allerlei (a vegetable medley) and Leipziger Lerche (a pastry filled with marzipan and jam) to global flavors from Asia, Africa, and the Middle East, Leipzig offers something to satisfy every palate and culinary craving.

As a city of music, literature, and cultural crossroads, Leipzig invites visitors to explore its rich history, vibrant arts scene, and dynamic urban landscape. Whether you're attending a concert at the Gewandhaus, browsing the bookshelves at the Leipzig Book Fair, or simply soaking up the atmosphere in one of its many cafes and parks, Leipzig offers a memorable experience that celebrates the power of creativity, imagination, and human connection.

Nuremberg: Medieval Majesty and Modern Resilience

With a history that spans over a thousand years, Nuremberg is a city that has played a significant role in shaping the cultural, economic, and political landscape of Europe.

At the heart of Nuremberg's medieval majesty is its well-preserved Altstadt, or Old Town, a labyrinth of cobblestone streets, half-timbered houses, and historic landmarks that transport visitors back in time. The centerpiece of the Old Town is the towering Kaiserburg, or Imperial Castle, which dates back to the 11th century and offers panoramic views of the city below. The castle's impressive fortifications, towers, and courtyards bear witness to Nuremberg's strategic importance as an imperial stronghold and seat of power during the Holy Roman Empire.

Nuremberg's medieval legacy is further evident in its iconic city walls and gates, which once served as a defensive barrier against invaders and marauders. The most famous of these gates is the Lorenzkirche, or St. Lorenz Church, a masterpiece of Gothic architecture that houses a wealth of medieval art and artifacts, including the renowned Angelic Salutation altarpiece by Veit Stoss.

But Nuremberg is more than just a city frozen in time; it is also a thriving modern metropolis with a resilient spirit that has endured through centuries of challenges and hardships. Despite being heavily damaged during World War II, Nuremberg has undergone extensive reconstruction and revitalization efforts, transforming it into a dynamic center of commerce, industry, and innovation.

Today, Nuremberg is known for its vibrant economy, with thriving sectors in manufacturing, technology, and research. The city is home to numerous multinational corporations, research institutions, and universities, making it a hub of innovation and entrepreneurship in southern Germany.

Nuremberg's cultural scene is equally vibrant, with theaters, museums, and galleries showcasing a diverse array of art, history, and performance. The Germanisches Nationalmuseum, one of the largest museums of cultural history in the world, offers a comprehensive overview of German art and culture from prehistoric times to the present day. The Nuremberg Opera House and the Nuremberg Symphony Orchestra provide world-class performances of opera, ballet, and classical music throughout the year, while the annual Nuremberg International Human Rights Film Festival highlights the city's commitment to social justice and human rights.

In addition to its cultural attractions, Nuremberg is known for its culinary delights, with a variety of restaurants, beer gardens, and street food stalls serving up delicious regional specialties and international cuisine. From traditional Franconian dishes like Nürnberger Bratwurst (grilled sausages) and Drei im Weggla (three sausages in a bun) to gourmet dining experiences and trendy cafes, Nuremberg offers something to satisfy every palate and culinary craving.

As a city of medieval majesty and modern resilience, Nuremberg invites visitors to explore its rich history, vibrant culture, and dynamic urban landscape. Whether you're wandering the streets of the Old Town, admiring the view from the Kaiserburg, or sampling the flavors of local cuisine, Nuremberg offers a memorable experience that celebrates its past, present, and future.

Stuttgart: Automotive Innovation and Swabian Hospitality

With a blend of modernity and tradition, Stuttgart offers visitors a fascinating glimpse into the heart of Germany's automotive industry and the warmth of its regional culture.

At the forefront of Stuttgart's identity is its status as a global hub for automotive engineering and innovation. The city is home to the headquarters of renowned automotive companies such as Mercedes-Benz and Porsche, which have played pivotal roles in shaping the automotive landscape for over a century. Visitors to Stuttgart can explore the Mercedes-Benz Museum and the Porsche Museum, both of which showcase the rich history, technological advancements, and iconic vehicles that have made these brands synonymous with luxury and performance.

In addition to its automotive prowess, Stuttgart is also known for its Swabian hospitality and rich cultural heritage. The Swabians, the region's indigenous population, are renowned for their warmth, generosity, and love of good food and wine. Visitors to Stuttgart can experience Swabian hospitality firsthand by dining at traditional restaurants known as "besenwirtschaften," where local winemakers serve their own wines alongside hearty Swabian dishes such as maultaschen (filled pasta pockets) and spätzle (egg noodles).

Stuttgart's cultural scene is equally vibrant, with theaters, museums, and galleries showcasing a diverse array of art, history, and performance. The Staatsoper Stuttgart, one of Germany's premier opera houses, offers world-class performances of opera, ballet, and classical music, while the Stuttgart Ballet is renowned for its innovative choreography and dynamic performances. The city's numerous museums, including the Staatsgalerie Stuttgart and the Kunstmuseum Stuttgart, house impressive collections of art spanning centuries and continents, providing visitors with a comprehensive overview of artistic expression.

Stuttgart's natural beauty adds to its charm, with lush parks, gardens, and vineyards dotting the cityscape. The Schlossgarten, a sprawling park in the heart of the city, offers tranquil green spaces, meandering pathways, and scenic vistas of the surrounding hills, providing residents and visitors alike with a peaceful retreat from urban life. The nearby Neckar River and Stuttgart's surrounding countryside offer opportunities for outdoor recreation such as hiking, cycling, and wine tasting, allowing visitors to immerse themselves in the region's natural splendor.

As a city of automotive innovation and Swabian hospitality, Stuttgart invites visitors to explore its dynamic blend of industry, culture, and natural beauty. Whether you're touring a cutting-edge automotive factory, savoring a glass of local wine at a traditional besenwirtschaft, or admiring masterpieces at a world-class museum, Stuttgart offers a memorable experience that celebrates the best of German engineering and hospitality.

German Art and Architecture: From Romanticism to Bauhaus

From the romantic landscapes of the 19th century to the innovative designs of the Bauhaus movement in the early 20th century, German art and architecture have left an indelible mark on the cultural landscape of Europe and beyond.

The roots of German art can be traced back to the Middle Ages, when illuminated manuscripts, woodcarvings, and religious paintings adorned churches and monasteries across the region. The Gothic period brought soaring cathedrals and intricate stone carvings, while the Renaissance ushered in a revival of classical forms and techniques, as seen in the works of artists like Albrecht Dürer.

But it was during the Romantic era of the 19th century that German art truly came into its own. Romanticism embraced emotion, nature, and the sublime, inspiring artists to explore themes of individualism, spirituality, and the supernatural. Painters such as Caspar David Friedrich captured the beauty and mystery of the natural world in their landscapes, while writers like Johann Wolfgang von Goethe and the Brothers Grimm tapped into the folk traditions and fairy tales of the Germanic past.

The 20th century brought seismic shifts in the world of German art and architecture, as the country grappled with the aftermath of two world wars and the rise of modernism. The Bauhaus movement emerged as a revolutionary force, advocating for a synthesis of art, craft, and technology in pursuit of functional and aesthetic purity. Founded by Walter Gropius in 1919, the Bauhaus school sought to break down the barriers between the fine arts and applied arts, producing iconic designs in architecture, furniture, and graphic design that would influence generations of artists and designers. The legacy of Bauhaus can be seen in the sleek lines and minimalist forms of modernist architecture, as well as in the functionalist approach to design that continues to shape our built environment today. Architects such as Ludwig Mies van der Rohe and Le Corbusier embraced the principles of Bauhaus, creating buildings that were simple, efficient, and responsive to the needs of the modern world.

But German art and architecture are not confined to the confines of any one movement or style. Throughout history, German artists and architects have drawn inspiration from a diverse range of influences, from the classical traditions of ancient Greece and Rome to the avant-garde experiments of the 21st century. Today, German art and architecture continue to evolve and thrive, with artists pushing the boundaries of expression and architects reimagining the built environment in response to the challenges and opportunities of the contemporary world.

In essence, German art and architecture represent a dynamic and ever-changing reflection of the cultural, social, and political forces that have shaped the nation's history and identity. From the romantic vistas of the Rhine Valley to the sleek lines of the Berlin skyline, German art and architecture invite us to explore the past, present, and future of a nation at the crossroads of creativity and innovation.

Music and Literature: German Contributions to World Culture

From the timeless compositions of classical composers to the profound insights of literary giants, German contributions to music and literature have enriched our lives and inspired generations of artists and thinkers.

In the realm of music, Germany boasts a rich tradition that spans a wide range of genres and styles. Classical music flourished in Germany during the Baroque, Classical, and Romantic periods, with composers such as Johann Sebastian Bach, Ludwig van Beethoven, and Wolfgang Amadeus Mozart leaving an enduring legacy of masterpieces that continue to be performed and revered around the world.

The 19th century saw the rise of the German Lied, or art song, a genre that combined poetry and music to express profound emotions and insights into the human condition. Composers such as Franz Schubert, Robert Schumann, and Johannes Brahms composed hundreds of Lieder, setting the poetry of Goethe, Heine, and other literary giants to music in works of exquisite beauty and depth.

In the 20th century, Germany continued to be a powerhouse of musical innovation, with composers such as Richard Strauss, Gustav Mahler, and Arnold Schoenberg pushing the boundaries of tonality and form. The advent of electronic music in the mid-

20th century brought new possibilities for sonic exploration, with pioneering artists such as Karlheinz Stockhausen and Kraftwerk revolutionizing the way we think about sound and composition.

German literature is equally rich and diverse, with a tradition that stretches back over a thousand years. The Middle Ages gave birth to epic poems such as the Nibelungenlied and the Minnesang tradition of courtly love poetry, while the Renaissance saw the emergence of humanist thinkers such as Johann Wolfgang von Goethe and Friedrich Schiller.

The 19th century was a golden age of German literature, with writers such as Johann Wolfgang von Goethe, Friedrich Schiller, and Heinrich Heine producing works of enduring significance and influence. Goethe's Faust, Schiller's William Tell, and Heine's Buch der Lieder are just a few examples of the literary masterpieces that emerged during this period, exploring themes of love, freedom, and the human condition with unparalleled depth and insight.

In the 20th century, German literature continued to flourish, with writers such as Thomas Mann, Hermann Hesse, and Franz Kafka gaining international acclaim for their probing explorations of identity, morality, and the nature of existence. The horrors of World War II and the Holocaust cast a long shadow over German literature, inspiring writers such as Günter Grass and Heinrich Böll to grapple with the moral and existential challenges of their time.

Today, German music and literature continue to thrive, with a new generation of artists and writers pushing the boundaries of creativity and expression in the digital age. From the experimental sounds of electronic music to the thought-provoking narratives of contemporary literature, German contributions to music and literature remain as vital and relevant as ever, inviting us to explore the depths of human experience and imagination.

Christmas Markets: Festive Traditions and Holiday Cheer

Welcome to the enchanting world of Christmas markets, where festive traditions and holiday cheer come alive in bustling town squares and cobblestone streets across Germany and beyond. These magical markets, known as Weihnachtsmärkte in German, have been a cherished part of European holiday celebrations for centuries, offering visitors a chance to experience the sights, sounds, and flavors of the season in a joyous and festive atmosphere.

The origins of Christmas markets can be traced back to the late Middle Ages, when towns and cities would hold seasonal fairs and markets to mark the advent of the Christmas season. Over time, these markets evolved into the beloved holiday traditions we know today, with vendors selling a wide array of goods and gifts, from handmade crafts and decorations to traditional foods and beverages.

One of the hallmarks of Christmas markets is their festive decorations, which transform town squares and historic landmarks into winter wonderlands of twinkling lights, evergreen garlands, and elaborately decorated Christmas trees. The scent of mulled wine, roasted chestnuts, and freshly baked gingerbread fills the air, enticing visitors to indulge in the culinary delights of the season.

In addition to food and drink, Christmas markets offer a variety of shopping opportunities, with vendors selling everything from handcrafted ornaments and toys to regional specialties and artisanal goods. Visitors can browse stalls filled with wooden toys, handmade candles, and intricately crafted decorations, finding unique and thoughtful gifts for loved ones back home.

But Christmas markets are more than just shopping destinations; they are also vibrant cultural events that bring communities together to celebrate the spirit of the season. Live music performances, festive parades, and traditional folk dances entertain crowds of all ages, while children delight in carousel rides, visits with Santa Claus, and storytelling sessions.

Each Christmas market has its own unique charm and character, reflecting the traditions and customs of its region. In Germany, cities like Nuremberg, Dresden, and Cologne are renowned for their iconic Christmas markets, which draw millions of visitors from around the world each year. In addition to their festive ambiance and holiday offerings, these markets also showcase local traditions and craftsmanship, providing a glimpse into the rich cultural heritage of the region.

Beyond Germany, Christmas markets can be found in cities and towns across Europe and even in other parts of the world, each offering its own interpretation of the holiday season. From the medieval charm of Prague's Old Town Square to the scenic beauty of Vienna's Rathausplatz, Christmas markets offer travelers a chance to experience the magic of the season in some of the world's most enchanting settings.

In essence, Christmas markets are a celebration of community, tradition, and the joy of giving, bringing people together to share in the spirit of the season and create cherished memories that last a lifetime. Whether you're sipping mulled wine by the fire, browsing stalls filled with festive treasures, or simply soaking up the festive atmosphere, Christmas markets are sure to fill your heart with holiday cheer.

Oktoberfest: Celebrating Bavarian Culture and Beer

Welcome to Oktoberfest, the world's largest and most famous beer festival, held annually in Munich, Bavaria, Germany. This iconic event is a celebration of Bavarian culture, tradition, and of course, beer. Oktoberfest dates back to 1810, when it began as a royal wedding celebration for Crown Prince Ludwig and Princess Therese of Bavaria. The festivities included horse races, parades, and, of course, plenty of beer. Over time, Oktoberfest evolved into the beloved event we know today, attracting millions of visitors from around the world each year.

The heart of Oktoberfest is the Theresienwiese, a sprawling fairground in central Munich that hosts the festival's famous beer tents, amusement rides, and attractions. The festival officially kicks off with the ceremonial tapping of the first keg by the Mayor of Munich, who declares, "O'zapft is!" (It's tapped!). This marks the beginning of two weeks of revelry, music, and merrymaking.

The beer tents at Oktoberfest are the main attraction, with each tent offering its own unique atmosphere, décor, and selection of beers. Traditional Bavarian bands entertain crowds with lively music and sing-alongs, while servers clad in traditional dirndls and lederhosen keep the beer flowing in massive steins known as Maßkrüge. Oktoberfest beer is brewed according to strict Bavarian purity laws and is typically a Märzen-style lager, known for its rich, malty flavor and amber hue.

In addition to beer, Oktoberfest offers a wide array of traditional Bavarian foods and delicacies to satisfy hungry revelers. From hearty dishes like weißwurst (white sausage), pretzels, and roast chicken to sweet treats like apple strudel and käsespätzle (cheese noodles), there's something to tempt every palate.

Beyond the beer tents, Oktoberfest boasts a variety of attractions and activities to entertain visitors of all ages. Thrill-seekers can enjoy rides on the festival's iconic Ferris wheel, roller coasters, and carnival games, while families can explore the colorful parades, folk dances, and traditional crafts on display.

Oktoberfest is not just a festival; it's a cultural phenomenon that embodies the spirit of Bavaria and the warmth of German hospitality. It's a time to come together with friends and strangers alike, to raise a stein in celebration of life, love, and the joy of being alive. So whether you're a seasoned Oktoberfest veteran or a first-time visitor, join us in Munich for a truly unforgettable experience filled with laughter, camaraderie, and of course, plenty of beer. Prost!

German Folklore and Fairy Tales: Stories That Transcend Time

German folklore is a rich tapestry of legends, myths, and fables that have been passed down through generations, shaping the cultural identity of the nation and inspiring countless writers, artists, and storytellers.

One of the most famous collectors of German folklore was the Brothers Grimm, Jacob and Wilhelm, who compiled and published a collection of fairy tales in the early 19th century. Their collection, known as "Grimm's Fairy Tales," includes beloved classics such as "Snow White," "Cinderella," and "Hansel and Gretel," as well as lesser-known tales like "Rumpelstiltskin" and "The Frog Prince." These timeless stories continue to enchant readers of all ages with their universal themes of love, bravery, and the triumph of good over evil.

But the Brothers Grimm were not the only ones to contribute to the rich tapestry of German folklore. Folklorists such as Johann Karl August Musäus and Ludwig Bechstein also collected and published collections of fairy tales and folk legends, preserving the oral traditions of the German people for future generations.

German folklore is populated by a diverse cast of characters, including witches, giants, dwarfs, and talking animals, each with their own unique powers and personalities. Many of these characters have become iconic symbols of German culture, such as the mischievous imp Rumpelstiltskin, the wise old grandmother in "Little Red Riding Hood," and the brave little tailor who outwits giants and dragons. In addition to fairy tales, German folklore also includes a wealth of legends and myths that have been passed down through the ages. These stories often draw inspiration from historical events, natural phenomena, and religious beliefs, offering insights into the cultural, social, and spiritual values of the German people.

One of the most famous German legends is that of the Lorelei, a beautiful siren who lures sailors to their doom with her enchanting song. According to legend, the Lorelei resides atop a steep cliff overlooking the Rhine River, where she sings her haunting melodies to passing ships, causing them to crash upon the rocks below. The legend of the Lorelei has inspired countless works of art, literature, and music, becoming a symbol of the allure and danger of the natural world.

German folklore is also rich in seasonal traditions and rituals, with festivals and celebrations marking the passage of time throughout the year. From the colorful costumes and parades of Carnival to the festive lights and decorations of Christmas, these traditions reflect the changing seasons and the rhythms of rural life in Germany.

In essence, German folklore and fairy tales are an integral part of the nation's cultural heritage, offering a window into the imagination and creativity of its people. Whether passed down through oral tradition or immortalized in print, these stories continue to resonate with audiences around the world, transcending time and geography to touch the hearts and minds of generations to come.

Castles and Palaces: Fairytale Architecture and Historical Significance

Germany is home to over 20,000 castles and palaces, making it one of the most castle-rich countries in the world. These impressive fortresses and residences vary in size, style, and purpose, ranging from imposing medieval strongholds to opulent Baroque palaces.

One of the most iconic German castles is Neuschwanstein Castle, located in the picturesque Bavarian Alps. Built by King Ludwig II in the 19th century, Neuschwanstein is a masterpiece of Romantic architecture, with its soaring turrets, ornate facades, and breathtaking mountain backdrop. The castle's fairytale appearance inspired Walt Disney's Sleeping Beauty Castle and continues to draw millions of visitors each year.

Another notable German castle is Heidelberg Castle, overlooking the historic city of Heidelberg on the banks of the River Neckar. Dating back to the 13th century, Heidelberg Castle is a prime example of Renaissance architecture, with its red sandstone walls, elegant courtyards, and sweeping views of the surrounding countryside. The castle's ruins have been immortalized in countless works of art and literature, symbolizing the beauty and resilience of the German spirit.

In addition to castles, Germany is also home to a wealth of magnificent palaces that once served as royal residences and centers of power. Sanssouci Palace, located in Potsdam near Berlin, was the summer palace of Frederick the Great, King of Prussia. Built in the Rococo style, Sanssouci is surrounded by lush gardens and terraces, offering a tranquil retreat from the bustle of city life.

Another notable palace is the Residenz in Munich, once the royal palace of the Bavarian monarchs. This sprawling complex boasts over 130 rooms, including opulent ballrooms, lavish chambers, and the stunning Antiquarium, one of the largest Renaissance halls north of the Alps. The Residenz is a testament to the wealth and power of the Bavarian rulers, who spared no expense in creating a palace fit for royalty.

But German castles and palaces are not just architectural marvels; they are also repositories of history, culture, and art. Many of these historic sites house impressive collections of artwork, furniture, and artifacts that offer insights into the lives and legacies of the people who inhabited them. From priceless paintings and tapestries to intricate sculptures and porcelain, these treasures provide a window into the past and a deeper understanding of Germany's rich cultural heritage.

In essence, German castles and palaces are more than just buildings; they are symbols of the nation's identity and aspirations, reflecting its tumultuous history and enduring legacy. Whether perched on a hilltop overlooking a medieval town or nestled in the heart of a bustling city, these architectural wonders continue to inspire awe and wonder, inviting visitors to step back in time and experience the grandeur of Germany's royal past.

Black Forest: Mystical Landscapes and Outdoor Adventures

Covering an area of approximately 6,000 square miles, the Black Forest, or Schwarzwald in German, is a captivating destination that has long captured the imagination of travelers and nature enthusiasts alike.

The Black Forest is named for its dense canopy of evergreen trees, which cast a dark shadow over the landscape and give the region its distinctive appearance. These towering trees, primarily spruce and fir, create a sense of mystery and enchantment, earning the forest its reputation as a place of legends and folklore.

One of the most iconic features of the Black Forest is its picturesque villages and towns, nestled among rolling hills and verdant valleys. These charming settlements are known for their half-timbered houses, traditional farmsteads, and quaint cobblestone streets, providing visitors with a glimpse into rural life in Germany.

The Black Forest is also home to a wealth of outdoor activities and adventures, making it a paradise for nature lovers and outdoor enthusiasts. Hiking trails crisscross the region, leading through dense forests, past tranquil lakes, and up to panoramic viewpoints. The famous Westweg, or West Trail, traverses the length of the Black Forest, offering hikers a chance to explore its diverse landscapes and natural beauty.

In addition to hiking, the Black Forest offers opportunities for cycling, mountain biking, and horseback riding, with numerous trails and routes to suit every skill level. Adventurous travelers can also try their hand at paragliding, rock climbing, and zip-lining, taking in breathtaking views of the forest canopy and surrounding countryside from above.

The Black Forest is also known for its rich culinary tradition, with hearty dishes and regional specialties that reflect the bounty of the land. Black Forest ham, smoked trout, and wild mushroom dishes are just a few examples of the delicious fare you can enjoy while exploring the region. And of course, no visit to the Black Forest would be complete without sampling a slice of the famous Black Forest cake, a decadent dessert made with layers of chocolate cake, whipped cream, and cherries.

But perhaps the most enchanting aspect of the Black Forest is its sense of tranquility and connection to nature. Whether you're wandering through ancient woodlands, picnicking by a babbling brook, or simply soaking in the serenity of a secluded glade, the Black Forest offers a chance to escape the hustle and bustle of modern life and reconnect with the rhythms of the natural world.

In essence, the Black Forest is a place of timeless beauty and wonder, where ancient forests and modern amenities coexist in perfect harmony. Whether you're seeking adventure, relaxation, or simply a change of scenery, the Black Forest invites you to embark on a journey of discovery and exploration in one of Germany's most enchanting regions.

Rhine Valley: Romantic Landscapes and Vineyard Scenery

Stretching from the Swiss Alps to the North Sea, the Rhine Valley is home to some of Europe's most breathtaking scenery, with rolling hills, craggy cliffs, and meandering riverbanks that have inspired poets, painters, and travelers for centuries.

The Rhine River, one of the longest and most important waterways in Europe, is the lifeblood of the Rhine Valley, winding its way through lush valleys and past picturesque towns and villages. Along its banks, you'll find countless castles, fortresses, and vineyards that tell the story of the region's rich history and cultural heritage.

One of the most iconic features of the Rhine Valley is its romantic castles and fortresses, perched atop rocky cliffs and overlooking the river below. These medieval strongholds, such as Burg Rheinfels, Marksburg Castle, and Schloss Stolzenfels, have stood for centuries as symbols of power, wealth, and resilience, offering visitors a glimpse into the region's turbulent past.

In addition to its castles, the Rhine Valley is also known for its picturesque vineyards, which produce some of Germany's finest wines. The steep slopes of the valley are covered with row upon row of grapevines, cultivated with care by generations of winemakers. The region is particularly famous for its Riesling wines, known for their crisp acidity, fruity flavors, and elegant aromas.

Wine tasting is a popular activity in the Rhine Valley, with numerous vineyards and wine estates offering tours and tastings for visitors. Whether you prefer dry whites, fruity reds, or sparkling sekt, you'll find a wine to suit your palate as you explore the scenic vineyards and picturesque wine villages of the region.

But the Rhine Valley is not just about castles and wine; it's also a paradise for outdoor enthusiasts and nature lovers. The region is crisscrossed by countless hiking and biking trails, leading through vineyards, orchards, and forests teeming with wildlife. Along the way, you'll encounter charming villages, historic landmarks, and panoramic viewpoints that offer sweeping vistas of the river and surrounding countryside.

In the summertime, the Rhine Valley comes alive with festivals and events celebrating the region's rich cultural heritage and agricultural traditions. From wine festivals and grape harvest celebrations to medieval fairs and boat races, there's always something happening in the Rhine Valley to delight visitors of all ages.

In essence, the Rhine Valley is a place of timeless beauty and romance, where the natural splendor of the landscape is complemented by the rich tapestry of history, culture, and tradition. Whether you're cruising down the river, hiking through the vineyards, or simply soaking in the scenery from a riverside café, the Rhine Valley invites you to experience the magic of one of Europe's most enchanting regions.

Bavarian Alps: Majestic Peaks and Alpine Wonders

Nestled in the southern part of Germany, the Bavarian Alps boast majestic peaks, verdant valleys, and crystal-clear lakes that form a stunning backdrop for outdoor exploration and mountain escapades.

At the heart of the Bavarian Alps lies the Zugspitze, Germany's highest peak, towering at an elevation of 9,718 feet (2,962 meters) above sea level. Dominating the skyline with its snow-capped summit, the Zugspitze offers panoramic views of the surrounding Alpine landscape, including the shimmering Eibsee Lake and the rugged peaks of the Wetterstein Mountains.

The Bavarian Alps are a paradise for outdoor enthusiasts, offering a wide range of activities to suit every taste and skill level. In the winter months, the region transforms into a winter wonderland, with world-class ski resorts such as Garmisch-Partenkirchen, Oberstdorf, and Berchtesgaden attracting skiers, snowboarders, and snow enthusiasts from near and far.

In the summertime, the Bavarian Alps come alive with a plethora of outdoor pursuits, from hiking and mountain biking to rock climbing and paragliding. The region is crisscrossed by a network of well-marked trails that lead through pristine forests, alpine meadows, and rugged mountain passes, providing endless opportunities for exploration and adventure.

One of the most popular hiking destinations in the Bavarian Alps is the Bavarian Forest National Park, Germany's first and largest national park. Covering an area of over 240 square miles (620 square kilometers), the park is home to diverse ecosystems, including ancient woodlands, mountain streams, and marshy meadows, which provide habitat for a variety of wildlife, including lynx, wolves, and golden eagles.

The Bavarian Alps are also known for their charming alpine villages and picturesque towns, where visitors can experience the region's rich cultural heritage and warm hospitality. Places like Garmisch-Partenkirchen, Mittenwald, and Oberammergau are renowned for their traditional Bavarian architecture, colorful frescoes, and lively festivals, which celebrate the customs, traditions, and folklore of the Alpine region.

No visit to the Bavarian Alps would be complete without sampling the region's hearty cuisine and local specialties. From savory dumplings and schnitzels to sweet treats like apple strudel and Kaiserschmarrn, there's no shortage of delicious fare to satisfy hungry travelers after a day of adventure in the mountains.

In essence, the Bavarian Alps are a playground for nature lovers and outdoor enthusiasts, offering a perfect blend of natural beauty, outdoor adventure, and cultural charm. Whether you're seeking adrenaline-pumping thrills on the slopes, serene moments of contemplation in the mountains, or simply a taste of Bavarian hospitality, the Bavarian Alps are sure to leave a lasting impression on all who visit.

German Festivals: From Wine Festivals to Beer Gardens

One of the most iconic German festivals is Oktoberfest, held annually in Munich, Bavaria. This legendary celebration traces its origins back to 1810 when Crown Prince Ludwig of Bavaria married Princess Therese of Saxony-Hildburghausen, and the citizens of Munich were invited to join in the festivities. Today, Oktoberfest is the largest beer festival in the world, attracting millions of visitors from around the globe who come to enjoy traditional Bavarian beer, hearty cuisine, and lively music in massive beer tents and beer gardens.

But Oktoberfest is just one of many beer festivals held throughout Germany each year. In addition to Munich's Oktoberfest, cities like Stuttgart, Nuremberg, and Berlin host their own beer festivals, featuring local brews, regional specialties, and live entertainment. These festivals offer a unique opportunity to experience the rich brewing heritage of Germany and immerse yourself in the convivial atmosphere of a traditional beer garden.

In addition to beer festivals, Germany is also known for its wine festivals, which celebrate the country's rich viticultural tradition and the bounty of its vineyards. The wine regions of Germany, such as the Moselle Valley, the Rhine Valley, and Franconia, host a variety of wine festivals throughout the year, showcasing local wines, culinary delights, and cultural performances. From the Rhine Wine Festival in Mainz to the Moselle Wine Festival in Bernkastel-Kues, these festivals offer a chance to sample some of Germany's finest wines and experience the unique terroir of each region.

But German festivals are not just about beer and wine; they also celebrate a wide range of cultural traditions, religious holidays, and seasonal events. From Carnival celebrations in Cologne and Düsseldorf to Christmas markets in Nuremberg and Dresden, there's always something happening in Germany to delight and entertain visitors of all ages.

In essence, German festivals are a vibrant expression of the country's rich cultural heritage and diverse regional identities. Whether you're raising a stein at Oktoberfest, sipping Riesling at a wine festival, or dancing in the streets during Carnival, German festivals offer a chance to experience the warmth, hospitality, and joie de vivre of the German people in all their glory.

German Fashion and Design: Style with Precision and Elegance

Germany has long been recognized as a global leader in the fashion and design industries, with a reputation for quality, attention to detail, and forward-thinking creativity.

One of the hallmarks of German fashion and design is its commitment to precision and craftsmanship. German designers are renowned for their meticulous attention to detail and their dedication to producing high-quality garments and products that stand the test of time. From finely tailored suits and couture gowns to sleek automobiles and cutting-edge furniture, German craftsmanship is synonymous with excellence and reliability.

In addition to precision, German fashion and design are also characterized by their understated elegance and refined aesthetic. German designers favor clean lines, minimalist silhouettes, and neutral color palettes, creating garments and products that exude sophistication and sophistication. Whether it's a beautifully tailored suit from Hugo Boss or a sleek, modern chair from Vitra, German design is all about marrying form and function to create objects of enduring beauty and utility.

Berlin, Germany's capital, has emerged as a vibrant hub of fashion and design, attracting designers, artists, and creatives from around the world. The city's diverse and dynamic cultural scene has fostered a spirit of innovation and experimentation, leading to the rise of cutting-edge fashion labels, avant-garde design studios, and underground art galleries. From the hip boutiques of Mitte to the edgy ateliers of Kreuzberg, Berlin is a city where creativity knows no bounds.

But German fashion and design are not limited to the runways of Berlin; they also have a strong presence on the global stage. German fashion brands like Adidas, Puma, and Birkenstock are internationally renowned for their sporty-chic aesthetic and innovative designs, while German automotive brands like BMW, Mercedes-Benz, and Porsche are synonymous with luxury, performance, and precision engineering.

In recent years, sustainability has also become a key focus of German fashion and design, with many designers and brands embracing eco-friendly materials, ethical production practices, and transparent supply chains. From upcycled textiles to zero-waste manufacturing techniques, German fashion and design are leading the way towards a more sustainable and socially responsible industry.

In essence, German fashion and design are a testament to the country's rich cultural heritage, innovative spirit, and commitment to excellence. Whether it's haute couture or streetwear, furniture or automobiles, German designers continue to push the boundaries of creativity and craftsmanship, shaping the way we live, work, and express ourselves in the modern world.

German Engineering: Precision and Innovation in Industry

German engineering is renowned for its meticulous attention to detail, cutting-edge technology, and relentless pursuit of excellence across a wide range of industries, from automotive manufacturing to aerospace, machinery, and beyond.

One of the key principles that sets German engineering apart is its commitment to precision. German engineers are known for their exacting standards and meticulous approach to design and manufacturing, ensuring that every component and product meets the highest quality standards. This dedication to precision is evident in everything from the intricate gears of a luxury watch to the flawless finish of a high-performance automobile.

Innovation is another hallmark of German engineering, with German engineers constantly pushing the boundaries of what is possible through research, development, and experimentation. Germany is home to some of the world's most innovative companies and research institutions, driving advancements in areas such as renewable energy, robotics, artificial intelligence, and autonomous vehicles.

The automotive industry is perhaps the most iconic example of German engineering prowess, with brands like Mercedes-Benz, BMW, Audi, and Volkswagen synonymous with luxury, performance, and reliability. German automakers are known for their cutting-edge technology, precision engineering, and meticulous attention to detail, producing some of the most advanced and sought-after vehicles on the market.

But German engineering extends far beyond the automotive sector, with Germany also leading the way in fields such as machinery and equipment manufacturing, electrical engineering, and aerospace. Companies like Siemens, Bosch, and Thyssenkrupp are global leaders in their respective industries, producing everything from industrial robots and power plants to elevators, escalators, and high-speed trains.

Germany's strong tradition of apprenticeship and vocational training also plays a key role in fostering a skilled workforce and nurturing the next generation of engineers and innovators. The country's dual education system combines classroom learning with on-the-job training, giving students the practical skills and real-world experience they need to succeed in the highly competitive field of engineering.

In recent years, sustainability and environmental stewardship have become increasingly important considerations in German engineering, with companies and policymakers alike placing a greater emphasis on green technology, energy efficiency, and eco-friendly manufacturing practices. From electric vehicles and renewable energy solutions to eco-friendly building materials and waste reduction strategies, German engineers are at the forefront of creating a more sustainable and environmentally conscious future.

In essence, German engineering is a testament to the country's tradition of excellence, innovation, and precision. Whether it's designing luxury automobiles, manufacturing state-of-the-art machinery, or pioneering breakthroughs in technology, German engineers continue to push the boundaries of what is possible, shaping the world we live in and driving progress and innovation on a global scale.

German Automotive Industry: A Legacy of Performance and Reliability

At the forefront of the German automotive industry are legendary manufacturers such as Mercedes-Benz, BMW, Audi, Volkswagen, and Porsche. These brands have earned international acclaim for their luxury, precision engineering, and cutting-edge technology. From sleek sedans and powerful sports cars to rugged SUVs and eco-friendly electric vehicles, German automakers offer a diverse range of vehicles that cater to every taste and preference.

One of the defining characteristics of the German automotive industry is its commitment to performance. German cars are synonymous with speed, agility, and superior handling, thanks to their advanced engineering and meticulous attention to detail. Whether it's the blistering acceleration of a Porsche 911, the smooth ride of a Mercedes-Benz S-Class, or the dynamic driving experience of a BMW M series, German cars are designed to deliver an exhilarating driving experience like no other.

But performance is just one aspect of what sets German cars apart. Another key factor is reliability. German automakers have built a reputation for producing vehicles that are built to last, with robust construction, durable materials, and rigorous testing ensuring that each car meets the highest standards of quality and durability. It's no wonder that German cars are often prized for their longevity and resale value, making them a smart investment for discerning buyers.

In addition to performance and reliability, German automakers are also at the forefront of automotive innovation, driving advancements in areas such as safety, connectivity, and sustainability. From cutting-edge driver-assistance systems and autonomous driving technology to eco-friendly hybrid and electric powertrains, German cars are at the forefront of shaping the future of mobility.

Germany's automotive industry is not just about manufacturing cars; it's also a vital engine of economic growth and innovation, employing millions of people and generating billions of dollars in revenue each year. The industry's supply chain encompasses a vast network of suppliers, manufacturers, dealerships, and service providers, all working together to ensure the continued success and competitiveness of German-made vehicles on the global market.

In essence, the German automotive industry is a testament to the country's engineering prowess, innovation, and commitment to excellence. With its legacy of performance and reliability, Germany continues to set the standard for automotive excellence, driving progress and innovation in the ever-evolving world of transportation.

Beer Culture: Brewing Traditions and Beer Gardens

Beer has long been an integral part of German culture, with a history dating back centuries and a rich tapestry of styles, flavors, and brewing techniques.

German beer culture is steeped in tradition, with breweries following time-honored methods passed down through generations. The Reinheitsgebot, or German Beer Purity Law, enacted in 1516, is one of the oldest food and beverage regulations in the world and stipulates that beer can only be brewed using water, barley, hops, and yeast. This purity law has played a significant role in shaping the German brewing tradition and ensuring the quality and integrity of German beer.

One of the most iconic symbols of German beer culture is the beer garden, a beloved institution where locals and visitors alike gather to enjoy cold brews, hearty cuisine, and warm camaraderie amidst lush greenery and shaded chestnut trees. Beer gardens have been a part of German social life for centuries, providing a welcoming and relaxed atmosphere for people of all ages to come together and unwind after a long day.

In addition to beer gardens, Germany is also home to a diverse array of beer styles, each with its own unique characteristics and regional variations. From crisp and refreshing lagers to rich and malty bocks, German brewers have mastered a wide range of beer styles, ensuring that there's something for everyone to enjoy.

Some of the most famous German beer styles include Pilsner, Weizenbier (wheat beer), Märzen, and Kölsch.

Beer festivals are another integral part of German beer culture, with cities and towns across the country hosting annual celebrations dedicated to the art of brewing and beer appreciation. The most famous of these festivals is Oktoberfest, held annually in Munich, where millions of visitors from around the world come to enjoy traditional Bavarian beer, music, and cuisine in massive beer tents and beer gardens.

But German beer culture is not just about drinking beer; it's also about appreciating the craftsmanship and heritage behind each brew. Many breweries offer guided tours and tastings, giving visitors a behind-the-scenes look at the brewing process and a chance to sample some of the finest beers Germany has to offer. Whether you're exploring the historic breweries of Bamberg, the scenic vineyards of Franconia, or the bustling beer halls of Berlin, German beer culture offers a wealth of experiences for beer enthusiasts and novices alike.

In essence, German beer culture is a celebration of craftsmanship, tradition, and community, where brewing traditions are honored, and beer gardens provide a welcoming haven for all who appreciate the simple pleasures of a cold beer on a warm summer day. So raise a stein, toast to good friends, and immerse yourself in the rich and flavorful world of German beer culture. Prost!

Wine Culture: Vineyard Tours and Riesling Delights

Welcome to the enchanting world of German wine culture, where centuries-old vineyards, picturesque landscapes, and exquisite Rieslings come together to create an unforgettable experience for wine enthusiasts and travelers alike. While Germany may be best known for its beer, its wine-producing regions are equally impressive, offering a diverse array of grape varieties, terroirs, and wine styles.

The heart of German wine country lies along the banks of the majestic Rhine and Moselle rivers, where steep vineyard slopes overlook the winding waterways below. These river valleys provide the perfect microclimate for growing grapes, with ample sunlight, moderate temperatures, and well-drained soils nurturing the vines to produce high-quality fruit.

One of the most iconic grape varieties of German wine culture is Riesling, renowned for its aromatic complexity, crisp acidity, and ability to reflect the unique terroir of each vineyard. German Rieslings range from bone-dry to lusciously sweet, with flavors of citrus, stone fruit, and minerality that captivate the palate and linger long after the last sip.

Vineyard tours are a popular way for visitors to immerse themselves in the rich history and winemaking traditions of Germany's wine regions. Guided tours offer insight into the cultivation and harvesting process, as well as the chance to sample a variety of wines straight from the source. Whether you're exploring the terraced slopes of the Moselle Valley or the sun-drenched hillsides of the Pfalz, each vineyard has its own story to tell and its own unique wines to savor.

But German wine culture is not just about Riesling; it also encompasses a wide range of other grape varieties and wine styles. From elegant Pinot Noirs to aromatic Gewürztraminers and crisp Müller-Thurgaus, German winemakers produce a diverse portfolio of wines that cater to every taste and occasion. Sparkling wines, known as Sekt, are also gaining popularity, with German producers crafting world-class bubblies that rival those from Champagne.

Wine festivals are another highlight of German wine culture, with towns and villages across the country hosting annual celebrations dedicated to the local wine industry. These festivals feature wine tastings, food pairings, live music, and traditional folk dancing, providing a festive atmosphere where locals and visitors can come together to celebrate the harvest and toast to the bounty of the vine.

In essence, German wine culture is a celebration of tradition, terroir, and the art of winemaking. Whether you're exploring the storied vineyards of the Rhine Valley, sipping Riesling in a cozy wine tavern, or attending a lively wine festival, the beauty and diversity of German wines are sure to captivate your senses and leave you longing for more. So raise a glass, savor the flavors, and embark on a journey through the enchanting world of German wine culture. Cheers!

German Etiquette and Customs: Navigating Social Norms

Navigating the intricacies of German etiquette requires an understanding of the values, behaviors, and expectations that underpin German society, allowing visitors and newcomers to engage respectfully and authentically with the local culture.

One of the cornerstones of German etiquette is punctuality. Germans take great pride in being on time and expect others to do the same. Whether it's a business meeting, social gathering, or dinner reservation, arriving promptly demonstrates respect for others' time and is considered a mark of professionalism and courtesy.

Another important aspect of German etiquette is greeting etiquette. When meeting someone for the first time, a firm handshake and direct eye contact are customary, accompanied by a polite greeting such as "Guten Tag" (Good day) or "Hallo" (Hello). Addressing people by their title and last name, especially in formal settings, is also common practice.

Table manners are also highly valued in German culture. When dining with others, it's customary to wait until everyone is seated and has been served before beginning to eat. Meals are typically enjoyed with utensils, with the fork in the left hand and the knife in the right. It's considered polite to keep your hands visible on the table while eating and to avoid resting your elbows on the table.

In social settings, Germans tend to value personal space and privacy. While they may be reserved with strangers, once a bond is formed, Germans are loyal and reliable friends. Building trust and mutual respect is essential for cultivating meaningful relationships in German society.

Gift-giving is another aspect of German etiquette that is deeply rooted in tradition. When presenting a gift, it's important to choose something of high quality and practical value. Gifts are typically opened upon receipt, and a handwritten thank-you note is appreciated as a gesture of gratitude.

When it comes to communication, Germans tend to value honesty, directness, and clarity. They prefer straightforward language and appreciate when others express their thoughts and opinions openly and honestly. Small talk is not as common in German culture as it is in some other cultures, so it's best to engage in substantive conversations rather than superficial chit-chat.

Respecting authority and following rules and regulations are also important aspects of German etiquette. Germans have a strong sense of order and discipline, and they expect others to adhere to established norms and guidelines in both public and private settings.

Overall, understanding and respecting German etiquette and customs are essential for building positive relationships and navigating social interactions with ease and grace. By embracing the values of punctuality, respect, honesty, and diligence, visitors and newcomers can fully immerse themselves in the rich tapestry of German culture and forge meaningful connections with the people they encounter along the way.

Efficiency and Punctuality: German Work Ethic in Practice

The German approach to work is deeply ingrained in the culture, reflecting a commitment to excellence, diligence, and precision that permeates all aspects of professional life.

One of the defining characteristics of the German work ethic is a strong emphasis on efficiency. Germans are known for their ability to streamline processes, optimize workflows, and achieve maximum productivity with minimal resources. This focus on efficiency is evident in every facet of German industry, from manufacturing and engineering to finance and technology.

Punctuality is another hallmark of the German work ethic. Germans place a high value on being on time and expect others to do the same. Whether it's arriving promptly for meetings, adhering to deadlines, or respecting schedules, punctuality is considered a sign of professionalism and reliability in the German workplace.

The concept of "Arbeitsmoral," or work ethic, is deeply rooted in German culture and history. Dating back to the Protestant Reformation, which emphasized the virtues of hard work, discipline, and thrift, the German work ethic has been shaped by centuries of cultural, religious, and philosophical influences. Today, it remains a central tenet of German identity and a source of national pride. Part of what drives the German work ethic is a strong sense of duty and responsibility. Germans take their work seriously and approach their professional obligations with a sense of purpose and dedication. Whether it's completing tasks to the best of their ability, going the extra mile to ensure quality and precision, or taking ownership of projects from start to finish, Germans take pride in their work and strive for excellence in everything they do. Another key aspect of the German work ethic is a commitment to lifelong learning and professional development. Germans place a high value on education and training, investing time and resources in continuous learning and skill development to stay competitive in a rapidly evolving global economy. From vocational training programs and apprenticeships to advanced degree programs and professional certifications, Germans are proactive about acquiring new knowledge and honing their skills to stay ahead of the curve.

In the German workplace, hierarchy and structure are important considerations. There is a clear chain of command, and decisions are often made through a collaborative process involving input from various stakeholders. Respect for authority, adherence to rules and procedures, and a focus on teamwork and collaboration are essential for maintaining harmony and efficiency in the workplace.

Overall, the German work ethic is characterized by a relentless pursuit of excellence, a commitment to efficiency and punctuality, and a strong sense of duty and responsibility. It is these values that have propelled Germany to become one of the world's leading economic powerhouses, driving innovation, productivity, and success in the global marketplace.

Environmentalism in Germany: Green Policies and Sustainability Efforts

From renewable energy initiatives to ambitious climate targets, Germany has emerged as a global leader in the fight against climate change and the promotion of sustainable development.

At the heart of Germany's environmental efforts is its ambitious energy transition, known as the "Energiewende." This initiative aims to transition the country's energy system away from fossil fuels and nuclear power toward renewable sources such as wind, solar, and biomass. Through a combination of government incentives, regulatory frameworks, and public-private partnerships, Germany has made significant strides in expanding its renewable energy capacity and reducing its carbon footprint.

One of the most iconic symbols of Germany's commitment to renewable energy is the Energiewende's flagship project, the "Energiewende Roadmap 2050." This comprehensive strategy outlines the steps necessary to achieve a carbon-neutral economy by 2050, including phasing out coal-fired power plants, increasing energy efficiency, and promoting the widespread adoption of electric vehicles. In addition to renewable energy, Germany has implemented a range of other green policies and sustainability initiatives aimed at protecting the environment and combating climate change. These include strict regulations on air and water quality, waste management and recycling programs, and measures to promote eco-friendly transportation and urban planning.

Germany's environmental efforts are also driven by a strong culture of environmental activism and grassroots engagement. From protests against deforestation and industrial pollution to campaigns for biodiversity conservation and wildlife protection, Germans are actively involved in advocating for environmental causes at the local, national, and international levels.

One of the most notable examples of grassroots environmental activism in Germany is the "Fridays for Future" movement, inspired by Swedish activist Greta Thunberg. This youth-led movement has mobilized millions of people across the country to demand urgent action on climate change and raise awareness about the importance of environmental sustainability.

In recent years, Germany has also emerged as a pioneer in sustainable urban development and green architecture. Cities like Berlin, Hamburg, and Freiburg are leading the way in implementing innovative green building practices, such as passive house design, green roofs, and sustainable materials, to reduce energy consumption and minimize environmental impact.

Overall, environmentalism in Germany is characterized by a multifaceted approach that encompasses government policies, community initiatives, and individual actions. By harnessing the power of renewable energy, embracing sustainable practices, and fostering a culture of environmental responsibility, Germany is paving the way for a greener, more sustainable future for generations to come.

Public Transportation: Efficiency and Accessibility Across the Country

From sleek high-speed trains to reliable regional buses and trams, Germany's public transportation system is renowned for its efficiency and convenience, making it a preferred choice for millions of commuters, tourists, and residents alike.

At the heart of Germany's public transportation network is the Deutsche Bahn (DB), the country's national railway company. With a vast network of tracks spanning over 33,000 kilometers, Deutsche Bahn operates a fleet of modern, high-speed trains that whisk passengers between major cities at speeds of up to 300 kilometers per hour. The InterCity Express (ICE) trains, in particular, offer a luxurious and comfortable travel experience, complete with onboard amenities such as Wi-Fi, dining cars, and spacious seating.

In addition to long-distance trains, Germany boasts an extensive network of regional and local trains that provide seamless connections between cities, towns, and rural areas. These RegionalExpress (RE) and RegionalBahn (RB) trains offer frequent service, affordable fares, and convenient access to destinations off the beaten path, making them a popular choice for commuters and leisure travelers alike. Complementing the rail network is an efficient network of buses, trams, and subways that serve urban and suburban areas across Germany. Cities like Berlin, Munich, and Hamburg boast extensive public transportation systems that include subway (U-Bahn), tram (Straßenbahn), and bus networks, providing residents and visitors with easy access to key attractions, neighborhoods, and business districts. Germany's public transportation system is also known for its accessibility and inclusivity. Many trains, buses, and stations are equipped with ramps, elevators, and other amenities to accommodate passengers with disabilities or reduced mobility. In addition, priority seating and designated areas for strollers and bicycles ensure that everyone can travel comfortably and safely.

Another key feature of Germany's public transportation system is its commitment to sustainability and environmental stewardship. With a focus on reducing carbon emissions and promoting eco-friendly modes of transportation, Germany has invested heavily in electrified trains, hybrid buses, and renewable energy sources to power its public transit infrastructure. Additionally, initiatives such as car-sharing programs, bike-sharing schemes, and pedestrian-friendly urban planning encourage alternative modes of transportation and reduce reliance on private cars.

Overall, Germany's public transportation system is a testament to the country's commitment to efficiency, accessibility, and sustainability. By offering a reliable and comprehensive network of trains, buses, and trams, Germany ensures that residents and visitors alike can travel conveniently and affordably while minimizing their environmental impact. Whether you're commuting to work, exploring a new city, or embarking on a scenic journey through the countryside, Germany's public transportation system has you covered.

German Technology: Innovations Shaping the Future

From automotive manufacturing and industrial automation to biotechnology and renewable energy, Germany is at the forefront of technological advancement, driving progress and pushing the boundaries of what's possible.

One of the key pillars of German technology is the automotive industry, which is renowned for its precision engineering, quality craftsmanship, and innovative design. German automakers such as Volkswagen, BMW, and Mercedes-Benz are synonymous with luxury, performance, and reliability, producing some of the world's most iconic and sought-after vehicles. From electric cars and autonomous driving technology to advanced safety features and eco-friendly innovations, German automakers are leading the charge toward a sustainable and connected future of mobility.

In addition to automotive technology, Germany is a global leader in industrial automation and manufacturing. Companies like Siemens, Bosch, and Festo are pioneers in the field of robotics, artificial intelligence, and smart manufacturing, revolutionizing production processes and driving efficiency and productivity to new heights. From automated assembly lines and 3D printing to predictive maintenance and digital twins, German companies are at the forefront of Industry 4.0, the fourth industrial revolution that is transforming the way goods are produced and distributed.

Germany's prowess in technology extends beyond the automotive and manufacturing sectors to areas such as biotechnology, renewable energy, and information technology. The country is home to world-class research institutions, such as the Fraunhofer Society and the Max Planck Society, as well as renowned universities and research centers that foster innovation and collaboration across disciplines. Breakthroughs in areas such as genome sequencing, renewable energy storage, and quantum computing are paving the way for a brighter and more sustainable future.

Another area where Germany excels in technology is renewable energy and sustainable development. The country has set ambitious targets for reducing carbon emissions and transitioning to renewable sources of energy, such as wind, solar, and biomass. Initiatives such as the Renewable Energy Sources Act (EEG) and the Energiewende have spurred investment in clean energy infrastructure and propelled Germany to the forefront of the global renewable energy transition.

In the realm of information technology, Germany is a powerhouse of innovation and entrepreneurship, with thriving startup ecosystems in cities like Berlin, Munich, and Hamburg. From fintech and e-commerce to cybersecurity and artificial intelligence, German startups are driving innovation and disruption in diverse industries, attracting investment and talent from around the world.

Overall, German technology is characterized by a relentless pursuit of innovation, a commitment to excellence, and a tradition of engineering prowess that spans centuries. Whether it's revolutionizing mobility, transforming manufacturing, or pioneering breakthroughs in science and research, Germany's technological innovations are shaping the future and making a lasting impact on the world.

German Influence on Global Affairs: Diplomacy and Leadership

With a history shaped by geopolitical shifts, economic prowess, and a commitment to multilateralism, Germany has emerged as a leading voice in global diplomacy, championing peace, stability, and cooperation among nations.

One of the defining features of Germany's influence on global affairs is its role as a founding member of the European Union (EU) and a driving force behind European integration. Since its inception, Germany has played a central role in shaping the EU's policies and institutions, advocating for closer political, economic, and social cooperation among member states. As the largest economy in Europe, Germany's leadership within the EU has helped to promote economic growth, strengthen democratic governance, and foster stability and security across the continent.

In addition to its role within the EU, Germany is also actively engaged in international diplomacy and foreign policy initiatives aimed at addressing global challenges and promoting peace and security around the world. As a member of key international organizations such as the United Nations (UN), NATO, and the G7, Germany contributes to efforts to resolve conflicts, combat terrorism, and advance human rights and democracy on a global scale.

Germany's commitment to diplomacy and leadership is further underscored by its role as a mediator and facilitator in international peacekeeping and conflict resolution efforts. From its involvement in the Iran nuclear deal to its participation in peace talks in the Middle East and Afghanistan, Germany has demonstrated a willingness to engage in dialogue and diplomacy to promote peaceful resolutions to complex geopolitical issues.

In recent years, Germany has also emerged as a champion of climate action and environmental sustainability on the global stage. Through initiatives such as the Paris Agreement and the United Nations Framework Convention on Climate Change (UNFCCC), Germany has committed to reducing greenhouse gas emissions, promoting renewable energy, and combating climate change on a global scale.

Another key aspect of Germany's influence on global affairs is its economic strength and leadership in international trade and finance. As one of the world's largest exporters and trading nations, Germany plays a vital role in shaping global economic trends and policies, driving innovation, and fostering economic development and prosperity around the world.

In conclusion, Germany's influence on global affairs is multifaceted and far-reaching, encompassing diplomacy, leadership, economic prowess, and a commitment to international cooperation and multilateralism. Whether it's promoting peace and stability, advancing environmental sustainability, or driving economic growth and development, Germany's contributions to global affairs are undeniable and continue to shape the course of history in the 21st century.

Epilogue

As we come to the end of our journey through the rich tapestry of Germany's history, culture, and influence, it's time to reflect on the insights gained and the lessons learned. Throughout this book, we've explored the diverse landscapes, vibrant cities, and fascinating traditions that make Germany a unique and captivating destination. From the majestic peaks of the Bavarian Alps to the romantic castles of the Rhine Valley, from the bustling streets of Berlin to the charming villages of the Black Forest, Germany's beauty and charm are boundless.

But beyond its picturesque landscapes and architectural wonders, Germany's story is one of resilience, innovation, and transformation. From the ancient tribes of the early Germanic peoples to the mighty Holy Roman Empire, from the rise and fall of Prussia to the devastation of two world wars, Germany has weathered countless challenges and emerged stronger and more determined than ever.

In the aftermath of World War II, Germany embarked on a path of reconstruction and reconciliation, laying the groundwork for the economic miracle that would transform it into an industrial powerhouse and a beacon of stability and prosperity in postwar Europe. The division of Germany into East and West during the Cold War was a painful chapter in the nation's history, but the peaceful reunification in 1990 marked a triumph of hope over adversity and paved the way for a new era of unity and progress.

Today, Germany stands as a global leader in technology, innovation, and sustainability, driving progress and shaping the future in fields ranging from automotive engineering and renewable energy to biotechnology and information technology. Its commitment to diplomacy, multilateralism, and international cooperation has made it a trusted partner and mediator in global affairs, while its rich cultural heritage and vibrant arts scene continue to inspire and captivate people around the world.

As we bid farewell to Germany, let us carry with us the lessons of its history, the beauty of its landscapes, and the warmth of its people. May we continue to explore, learn, and appreciate all that this remarkable country has to offer, and may its legacy of resilience, innovation, and unity serve as a source of inspiration for generations to come. Until we meet again, auf Wiedersehen, Germany.

Made in United States
Orlando, FL
29 January 2025